UNDERSTANDING THE AFRICAN PHILOSOPHICAL CONCEPT BEHIND THE "DIAGRAM OF THE LAW OF OPPOSITES"

UNDERSTANDING THE AFRICAN PHILOSOPHICAL CONCEPT BEHIND THE "DIAGRAM OF THE LAW OF OPPOSITES"

YOSEF ben-JOCHANNAN

with EVELYN WALKER, DOROTHY LEE COBB, and CALVIN BIRDSONG

Black Classic Press
Baltimore

UNDERSTANDING THE AFRICAN PHILOSOPHICAL CONCEPT BEHIND THE "DIAGRAM OF THE LAW OF OPPOSITES"

First published by Alkebu-lan Book Associates

Published 2005
by Black Classic Press

Library of Congress Card Catalog Number: 2004117965

ISBN 1-57478-035-2

Cover art by Michelle D. Wright, rendered from
the original cover by Yosef ben-Jochannan

Printed by BCP Digital Printing
An affiliate company of Black Classic Press

UNDERSTANDING THE AFRICAN PHILOSOPHICAL CONCEPT BEHIND THE "DIAGRAM OF THE LAW OF OPPOSITES"

- by -

Author: Yosef ben-Jochannan, Visiting Professor of History,

Co-Authors: Evelyn Walker, Dorothy Lee Cobb and Calvin Birdsong - candidates for the Master's Degree in Africana Studies, etc.; Africana Studies and Research Center, Cornell University, Ithaca, New York

OTHER WORKS BY THE AUTHOR, AND WITH CO-AUTHORS

We The Black Jews [pamphlet in Spanish, Puerto Rico, 1938; Spain, 1949]
The Rape Of Africa, And The Crisis In Angola [pamphlet in Portuguese and English, Ghana, 1958]
An African Nationalist View Of Black Power [pamphlet, article in Fall Issue of New York CORE's publication, 1966]

Works for children - Grade Four through Twelve, by W.H. Sadlier Company, New York, N.Y., 1969

Africa: The Land, The People, The Culture [co-authors: Y. ben-Jochannan, Ph.D., K. Webb, Ph. D., and H. Brooks, Ph. D.
Southern Lands [ibid, etc.]
Southern Neighbours [ibid, etc.]

Works published by Alkebu-lan Books Associates - a subsidiary of Alkebu-lan Foundation, New York, N.Y.

Black Man Of The Nile [1st Edition 1969, 1970 5th impression]
African Origins Of The Major "Western Religions", 1970, Vol. I
Africa: Mother Of "Western Civilization", 1971
The Black Man's North And East Africa [co-authors: Y. ben-Jochannan and George E. Simmonds], 1972
Black Man Of The Nile And His Family, 1972 [69 Ed./Rev./Enl'gd.]
Cultural Genocide In The Black And African Studies Curriculum, 1973
The Black Man's Religion: The Myth Of Genesis And Exodus, And The Exclusion Of Their African Origin, 1974, Vol. II and III
A Chronology Of The Bible: Challenge To The Standard Version, 1974

THE AUTHOR AND CO-AUTHORS

Yosef ben-Jochannan

Evelyn Walker

Calvin Birdsong

Dorothy Lee Cobb

HE LEARNT, TAUGHT, AND PREACHED A "BLACK THEOLOGY;" AND BELIEVED IN A "BLACK MESSIAH" FOR HIS BLACK PEOPLE

It is not the length of life that counts;
not how long we live, but how well.

OBSEQUIES

Above And Beyond The Limits Of A "DEDICATION"
In HONOURED SACRED MEMORIUM To OUR OWN
DEPARTED PROPHETIC LEADER AND SAINT...

JOMO IREGI
["James Holloman"],

THE REVEREND JAMES HOLLOMAN

1930 - 1975

Saturday, January 25, 1975 - 11:00 AM

United Missionary Baptist Church
18th at Minnesota Street, Middletown, Ohio

Who Always Reminded Us That: "TODAY IS THE LAST DAY FOR THE FIRST ACT."

The Greeks were not the authors of Greek Philosophy, but the people of North Africa, commonly called the Egyptians [George G. M. James, STOLEN LEGACY, New York, 1954; from title page and front cover].

OFFERING:

Yosef ben-Jochannan, Prelude...vi - vii

Glossary...viii - ix

Yosef ben-Jochannan, Lecture Title: Understanding The African Philosophical Concept Behind The "Diagram Of The Law Of Opposites"...viii

Yosef ben-Jochannan, Origin, Materialism, Mankind And Divinity...1 - 21

Evelyn Walker, The Law Of Opposites: An Interpretation...22 - 27

Dorothy Lee Cobb, The Cognitive Path...28 -37

Calvin Birdsong, Reflections On The Winter Solstice...38 - 45

Yosef ben-Jochannan, Postscript To The "Final Papers" Of Walker, Cobb And Birdsong... 46 - 53

Yosef ben-Jochannan, Conclusion...54 - 61

Indexed Citations Of Sources In The Textbook [Y. ben-Jochannan's BLACK MAN OF THE NILE AND HIS FAMILY]...62 - 63

ILLUSTRATIONS:

The "Diagram of Opposites" and "The Four Qualities and Four Elements"...1
Chronological List of the Nile Valley [Egyptian] Dynasties...3
Scene From The Herculaneum Worship Of Isis...8
Chronological List Of The Subordinate Lodges Of The Grand Lodge Of Luxor...9
Map Of The Nile Valley And Great Lakes Region: B.C.E. - C.E....10
Graphic Reproduction of the so-called "Rosetta Stone"...12
Map Of Alkebu-lan And Surrounding Continents - ca. 1236 - 600 B.C.E....15
Map Of Africa, 1688 C.E. [with ancients names included]...16
Subordinate Lodges Of The Grand Lodge Of Luxor, etc....49
Ethiopians, Twas/Hutus ["Pygmies"], Egyptian, etc. or "Negroes"...50
Diagram Of The Four Qualities And Four Elements...51
Science News of the Week: Ethiopia yields oldest human fossils...57
Thick Lips, Broad Nose, Woolly Hair, Black Skin; but not "Negroes" - "Caucasians"?...58

Note of acknowledgment: Appreciation to the Director, Administration Staff and General Student Body of AFRICANA STUDIES and RESEARCH CENTER is warmly extended by the Professor and Students of Course: AS and RC - 510, if for no other reason than your encouragement; particularly when it seemed that because of finance this volume would not be published minus a Grant.

There are many added footnotes to the "Essay" which none of the Students had when they were preparing their "FINAL PAPERS". They are specially for the readers understanding of the text.

An Essay

UNDERSTANDING THE AFRICAN PHILOSOPHICAL CONCEPT BEHIND THE "DIAGRAM OF THE LAW OF OPPOSITES" [1]

Lecture by Visiting Professor of History Yosef ben-Jochannan, Africana Studies and Research Center, Cornell University, Ithaca, New York

Course: AS and RC - 510
HISTORIOGRAPHY and SOURCE

for
Undergraduate Seniors and Graduate Students Seminar

Director: Prof. James Turner
Division Chairman: Prof. Congress Mbata

Due date: December 13, 1974

1. The following "Prelude" and "Glossary" [on pages vi - vii and viii - ix] were added to the Essay [pages 1 - 21] by Professor ben-Jochannan as an aid to the reading public. None of the Students was privileged to this information before the completion of the "FINAL PAPERS" [page 22 through 45].

PRELUDE: by Y. ben-Jochannan.

In dealing with AFRICAN-AMERICAN [Black] STUDENTS in the major EUROPEAN AMERICAN [White] INSTITUTIONS OF HIGHER LEARNING at campuses all over the United States of America, particularly those engaged in "AFRICAN" and/or "BLACK STUDIES," I found a serious lack of basic knowledge of ancient history in every discipline where the subject of "AFRICA" and "AFRICANS" is involved. This observation becomes fantastically alarming when one examines the history of MEDICINE, SCIENCE, MATHEMATICS, PHILOSOPHY, ART ENGINEERING, LAW, ASTRONOMY, ASTROLOGY, THEOLOGY, etc. ad infinitum. Why? Because it is mostly within these disciplines that AFRICAN-AMERICANS have been told for the last two centuries that they and their ancestors of "AFRICA" were never involved. And it is also in these areas they found that each one's LIFE is governed daily; even the promise of a "LIFE AFTER DEATH" in the OLD TESTAMENT and NEW TESTAMENT [any version].

In this volume it is with the basic laws of SCIENCE related to the PHILOSOPHICAL CONCEPTS upon which the "DIAGRAM OF THE LAW OF OPPOSITES" [created and developed b the Africans of the Nile Valley and Great Lakes High-Cultures] my graduate students have been introduced; they in turn indicated their understanding of the materials. And although the student "FINAL PAPERS" are of the nature of virgin investigation; it will be obvious to all that it is not impossible for all AFRICAN-AMERICAN STUDENTS of the 20th Century C.E. to become AUTHORITIES on their ancestors glorious contribution to their own people, and to the world gener ally.

I carefully admitted among the students one Senior UNDERGRADUATE, Kim Bressan whose "FINAL PAPER" is omitted because of academic technicality, although my course was designed for "GRADUATE STUDENTS" in the field of "AFRICAN STUDIES and RESEARCH". Agai this only validates my earlier conviction that under the correct method of instruction, combine with convincing interest in the nature of the subject matter, <u>any college student on any grade level can be taught any LIBERAL ARTS subject.</u> Thus each of the following student's FINAL PAPER is truly reflective of the "HIGH STANDARD" required by the Director, Administrators and Faculty of AFRICANA STUDIES and RESEARCH CENTER of Cornell University, Ithaca, New York. Director James Turner's leadership, so far as I am concern, along with his resear oriented faculty members who support such leadership, certainly reflected in the result of each of the FINAL PAPERS.

I am futher convinced that this effort will set a pattern for future professors and students engaged in the field of "AFRICANA [Black] STUDIES" all over the United States of

America. But it is my fervent hope that Africana Studies be equally taught in the future with emphasis on apprenticeship between RESEARCHER and STUDENT, and not solely between PROFESSOR and STUDENT. For I have experienced that STUDENTS are very much comfortable searching into their ANCESTRAL PAST and being astonished at his or her discoveries, also having their work criticized on the spot by the RESEARCHER - who at the same instance could bring to their attention other basic [primary and secondary, etc.] sources that would enhance the authenticity of each STUDENT-RESEARCHER'S work.

Uncovering the sources and artifacts for the FINAL PAPERS shown in this volume proved to have been the GREATEST ACHIEVEMENT of this course; not that there was no excitement in the LECTURES that were presented each Tuesday of the Semester; but due to the fact that the STUDENTS themselves were emotionally involved in the meaningful experiment whereby they were producing their own original studies without having to be in FEAR that the possibility of an "F" grade, or even an average "C" grade, hanged over their heads, should they have failed to produce ONE PAPER alone upon which their entire experience in the course was based. Thus, although the "FINAL PAPER" weighed heavily on the outcome of their FINAL GRADE, it only accounted for FIFTY PERCENT of the TOTAL GRADE for the entire semester's overall work [see page 17 for outline of total "requirements" for this course].

Most of all; the STUDENTS confidence of being able to CRITICIZE their own professor's work without any PENALTY hanging over them was another plus in their ability to perform at their very best. Thus from the "INTRODUCTION" on page 1 following, to the end of my critical analysis and hypothesis on "ORIGIN, MATERIALISM, MANKIND AND DIVINITY," etc. philosophical concept on page 16 - including the " FINAL PAPER REQUIREMENTS" on page 17, along with the very much "EXTENDED BIBLIOGRAPHY" on pages 18 through 21 - everyone of these STUDENTS were introduced to works they would never have known at this level of their educational experience the standard type of EUROPEAN and EUROPEAN-AMERICAN [White] STUDIES afford any kind of STUDENT today. The tragedy of it all is in the fact that AFRICAN-AMERICAN STUDENTS cannot expect anything different in the average so-called "NEGRO COLLEGES" anywhere in these United States of America; all, or at least most, of them having adopted everyone of the STANDARDS established in "WHITE ACADEMIA" as being "AUTHORITATIVE" in respect to the "AFRICAN [Black] EXPERIENCE" throughout the so-called "NEW WORLD" - the Caribbean Islands and the Americas, and even in ALKEBU-LAN [the Greeks so-called "Africa"]. The ancient motto - "MAN KNOW YOURSELF" - is certainly expressed in these STUDENTS' "FINAL PAPERS" we are about to read in the following pages - 22 through 45.

GLOSSARY [according to appearance in the reading text]: by Y. ben-Jochannan.

High-Culture: the equivalent of "civilization" without the racist connotation of anyone being "uncivilize."

Meröe: an African nation of antiquity located in part of what is today called "Sudan."

Dynasty: a period or reign by one person, group or family [see page 3 for list of Egyptian Dynasties according to chronology in years].

Transmutation: the process of changing form from the physical man into an unseen Being or God through Death and Resurrection.

Deification: the process of making Man GODLIKE, SAINT, PROPHET, while He is still a mer MORTAL on Earth, etc.

Deity: any GOD of any RELIGION, or any ONE and/or THING which people worship.

Christ: from the Greek word "CRYSTOS" or English word "ANOINTED" - Jesus "the Christ".

Lodge: a name of a PLACE or CENTER of learning [university] of antiquity that had its first beginning along the Nile Valley banks and Great Lakes area of Alkebu-lan.

Israelites: a misnomer for Haribu or Hebrew people which gave them a national identity befor they actually came into being as a nation called "Israel."

Hieroglyphics: a form of picture writing [see page 12]; the most ancient.

Osirica: the system of learning and devotion of Alkebu-lan dedicated to God - OSIRIS, the Firs Risen Christ ever mentioned in recorded history anywhere.

Alkebu-lan: the original name of the continent the Greeks renamed "AFRICA" [see page 16].

Rosetta Stone: a tablet of stone Europeans stole from Alkebu-lan's Ta-Merry containing on its surface Hieroglyphic, Hieratic and Greek scripts relative to Pharaoh Ptolemy IVth used to open the secret of many of the indigenous Africans of Ta-Merry's history, r ligion, science and other information from the teachings of the Mysteries System.

Christian Bible or New Testament: originally the KOINÊ BIBLE; began ca. 50 C.E. [A.D.] an completed ca. 100 C.E.

Hebrew Bible or Old Testament: originally the PENTATEUCH [Comesh, Torah, etc.]; began c 700 B.C.E. [B.C.] and completed ca. 500 B.C.E.

Moslem Bible:originally the QUR'AN [Koran], a set of poems and commentaries [allegedly] b AL'LAH; began ca. 710 C.E. [A.D. or 88 A.H. - the Year of the Hejira] and completed ca. 760 C.E. [A.D. or 138 A.H. 1 A.H. - the Year Mohammet ibn Abdullah, the "only founder-prophet of Islam,"established this religious outgrowth of Judaism and Christianity at the Oasis Of Yathrib near the City of Medina, having had to flee "Mecca" [the Moslems "Holy City"] to save his life in ca. 622 C.E. or 1 A.H.

Ra, Thoth, Aten, etc.: Nile Valley and Great Lakes African GODS, the forerunners of the GOI of Judaism, Christianity and Islam, etc.

Soul: the INNER-SELF or that which supposedly leave the body following death, sometimes cal ed "breath of life;" the traveller in resurrection.

Ankh: the Nile Valley and Great Lakes "African" symbol of the KEY OF LIFE [see page 30], forerunner of the "CHRISTIAN CROSS" or "CRUX ANSATA."

Delta or △: a letter in the Greek alphabet [see page 31]; in this volume a symbol representing the FEMALE VAGINA used in PHALLICISM or PHALLIC WORSHIP.

Pythagoras: a Greek of ca. 450 B.C.E. whom Diogenes Laertius said was responsible for teaching his fellow Greeks the mathematical concepts he learnt from the Africans of the Mysteries System in Ta-Merry, and which we call "THE PYTHAGOREAN THEORY."

Winter Solstice: that time in the year when Africans celebrated the Vernol Equinox.

Pygmies: a European colonialist and racist jargon created and designed to degrade the Twa and/or Hutu [ancient Sybenetos] people of Central Alkebu-lan [see pages 50 and 58].

Slave Trade: the dastardly business of transporting Africans across the Atlantic Ocean ["Middle Passage"] as a commerical commodity from its beginning in ca. 1506 C.E. with Rev. [later Bishop] Bartolome de LasCasas, the King and Queen of Spain, His Holiness the Pope and other dignitaries of the Roman Catholic "Christian" Church - the initiators. This does not exclude the Slave Trade by the Arabs of Asia that began about 400 years before the Europeans' across the Red Sea and Indian Ocean.

Caucasian: said to be a "RACE OF PEOPLE" [European and European-American] that originated at the foothills of the Caucasus Mountains between Asia and Europe [see page 58].

Negro: a racist term created by the Portuguese slavemasters and traders in the 16th or 17th Century C.E. [see Richard Moore, THE WORD NEGRO, ITS ORIGIN AND EVIL USE, New York, 1961; also Negroland, the accompanying word that generally appeared on European maps of the same period, see Y. ben-Jochannan, BLACK MAN OF THE NILE AND HIS FAMILY, pages 400 and 402, etc.].

Hamite: an equally racist type of name from the Old Testament's allegorical story about Noah and his Sons relative to the so-called "GREAT DELUGE" or "GREAT FLOOD." In this story the myth of "RACIAL DIFFERENCE" supposedly began; from which the so-called "NEGRO" was created by a "CURSE" placed upon them by Noah through their ancestor "HAM," the father of the "CANAANITES" - who gave birth to the "NEGROES" [see R. Graves and R. Patai, HEBREW MYTHS..., etc., MacGraw-Hill, New York, 1961, and Y. ben-Jochannan, BLACK MAN OF THE NILE AND HIS FAMILY, page 13, and equally the entire details from page 11 through 13].

Equilibrium: a state of Being, Oneness, Unity or Cause, according to theological concepts.

Monotheism: the concept or belief in a solitary GOD above all other Gods; originally preached by Pharaoh Akhenaten [Amenhotep IVth] over one hundred years before the birth of the African Hebrew [Israelite] Prophet named "Moses," whom Judaeo-Christian and Islamic theologians gave credit for its origin.

Polytheism: the concept of belief in plural GODS who rule in conjunction with an overseer type of God-head.

God: the male Deity - like Ywh, Jesus "the Christ," Al'lah, Oledumare, Voodum, etc.

Goddess [Godesse or Godess]: the female Deity - like Isis, Vashti, Mary, Al'lat, et al.

INTRODUCTION: by Y. ben-Jochannan.

"Authority" and "Validity," to me, are synonymous with "Power" and "Truth". But is there any "AUTHORITY, VALIDITY, POWER" and/or "TRUTH" inherent in a "DOCTOR" of anything whatsoever, and more specifically in AFRICAN [Black] HISTORY and CULTURE, when such has been awarded to an AFRICAN [Black] PERSON by EUROPEAN or EUROPEAN-AMERICAN [White] controllers of the institutions granting the DEGREE? The answer inherent in this question is equally the same as it is in the contradictions we find in the HISTORIOGRAPHY OF AFRICAN HISTORY AND CULTURE. For as most of the so-called BLACK STUDIES BOOKS and/or AUTHORITIES are still European and European-American in origin; and this is providing we are even considering any AFRICAN [Black] SCRIBE and/or HISTORIAN as such in BLACK and also WHITE institutions, we still continue requiring that the same "YARD STICK" [standard] used for measuring excellence of European and European-American [WHITE/SEMITIC] scholars be equally applied to African, African-American and African-Caribbean [BLACK] scholars. This is the major dilemma; the inherent inconsistency in it being the MASTERS' descendants and the SLAVES' descendants having the same interpretation of the relationship that existed between their ancestors during the INFAMOUS SLAVE TRADING and SLAVE PLANTATION days; and before this, even back to the period when Egyptians, Nubians, Ethiopians, Puanits, etc. [AFRICANS and/or BLACKS] began introducing the Europeans of Greece and Rome to "CIVILIZE LIVING"; also the Carthagenians and Moors, who later repeated the "CIVILIZING MISSIONS" to the southern Europeans around the IIIrd Century B.C.E. and VIIIth Century C.E. respectively.

The following highlights are designed to stimulate the Graduate Students' mind to a much clearer understanding, from a HISTORIGRAPHICAL DIMENSION, just why "AFRICANA [BLACK] STUDIES" must suffer the STEPCHILD relationship it has encountered since its quasi acceptance during the 1960's C.E. in BLACK and/or WHITE controlled "Institutions Of Higher Learning" up until the present. But more importantly, it should make the Graduate Student understand why serious effort must be given to ORIGINAL SOURCES and DOCUMENTS in preference to COMMENTARIES, HYPOTHETICAL ANALYSIS and "GOD'S SACRED WORKS BY HIS INSPIRED SCRIBES" type of allegories and myths we have had to rely upon for our "FACTS" about African [BLACK] People, Places and Properties over the past four hundred [400] years or more to date. But the Graduate Student must realize that...

> THE SOLUTION IS IN THE HANDS OF
> THE MOST COMPETENT SCHOLAR
> WHO IS DEDICATED TO AFRICANA
> STUDIES AND RESEARCH; ALONE....

ORIGIN, MATERIALISM, MANKIND AND DIVINITY: by Y. ben-Jochannan

If we were asked; at what point would you begin a lecture on the "Deification Of Man"? I would have had to explain the answer in terms of my understanding of the following forces that made the difference between myself and all of the other living creatures around and about me. Thus,I could have said it in the following symbol, which is otherwise known as:

THE FOUR QUALITIES and FOUR ELEMENTS

of the

DIAGRAM OF THE PRINCIPLE OF THE LAW OF OPPOSITES.

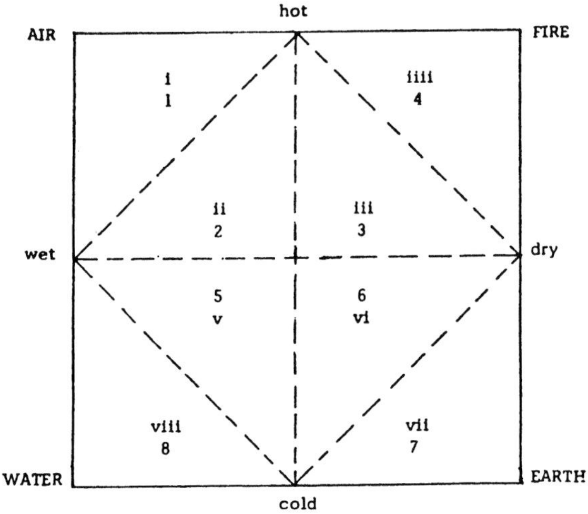

The Four Elements: AIR, FIRE; WATER, EARTH

The Four Qualities: HOT, DRY; WET, COLD

THE 8 EQUAL △ POLE STARS

The theory in the above "Diagram" comes from my earliest ancestors who inhabited the banks along the Blue and White Nile and Great Lakes High-Cultures that reached their zenith in Ta-Merry, Ta-Nehisi, Itiopi, Meröe and Puanit. This teaching has been mistakenly assigned solely to the Ta-Merrians [Egyptians] and Ta-Merry [Egypt] by so-called Western Egyptologists and other European and European-American "academicians" who can only relate it scientifically to the qualities. But there is no doubt that before the Ist Dynasty in ca. 3100 B.C.E. or ca. 4100 B.C.E. [depending upon whose chronological chart one uses, as shown on the following page], probably as early as 5100 B.C.E., it was considered the symbol that depicted the INNER SELF

1. See Yosef ben-Jochannan's AFRICA: MOTHER OF WESTERN CIVILIZATION, pages 384 - 38

our African ancestors spoke about with respect to the...

"TRANSMUTATION [migration] OF THE SOUL",

which is still the basic prerequisite they told us must be accomplished in order to realize the...

"DEIFICATION OF MAN".

DATES OF EGYPTIAN DYNASTIES BY EUROPEAN "AUTHORITIES IN EGYPTOLOGY" COMPARED TO MANETHO'S ORIGINAL WORKS [1]

Period or DYNASTY	Manetho (280 B.C) DATE	Champollion-Figeac (?A.D) DATE	Lepsius (1858AD) DATE	Brugsh (1877AD) DATE	Mariette (?AD) DATE
	First Book				
I	9K, 253Y	5,867*	3,892*	4,400*	5,004*
II	9K, 302Y	5,615	3,639	4,133	4,751
III	9K, 214Y	5,318	3,338	3,966	4,449
IV	8K, 284Y	5,121	3,124	3,733	4,235
V	9K, 248Y	4,673	2,840	3,566	3,951
VI	6K, 203Y	4,225	2,744	3,300	3,703
VII	70K, 0Y, 70D	4,222	2,592	3,100	3,500
VIII	27K, 146Y	4,147	2,522	?	3,500
IX	19K, 409Y	4,047	2,674**	?	3,358
X	10K, 185Y	3,947	2,565**	?	3,249
XI	192K, 2300Y, 70D	3,762	2,423	?	3,064
XII	7K, 160Y	3,703	2,380	?	2,851
XIII	?	3,417	2,136	2,235	?
XIV	76K, 184Y	3,004	2,167	?	2,398
XV	?	2,520	2,101	?	2,214
XVI	32K, 518Y	2,270	1,842	?	?
XVII	86K, 151Y	2,082	1,684	?	?
XVIII	16K, 263Y	1,822	1,581	1,700	1,703
	Second Book				
XIX	7K, 209Y	1,473	1,443	1,400	1,462
XX	12K, 135Y	1,279	1,269	1,200	1,288
XXI	7K, 130Y	1,101	1,091	1,100	1,110
XXII	9K, 126Y	971	961	966	980
XXIII	4K, 28Y	851	787	766	810
XXIV	1K, 6Y	762	729	733	721
XXV	3K, 40Y	718	716	700	715
XXVI	9K, 150Y, 6M	674	685	666	665
XXVII	8K, 124Y, 4M	524	525	527	527
XXVIII	1K, 6Y	404	525	?	406
XXIX	4K, 20Y, 4M	398	399	399	399
XXX	3K, 38Y	377	378	378	378
	Third Book				
XXXI***	?????????	399	340	340	340

* Note that the "AUTHORITIES" disagree as much as 1,000 years difference.
** These dates only prove the extent to which Lepsius was confused in his work.
*** Manetho did not complete this Dynasty's listing; he died before its termination in approximately 324 C.E. He actually did not list it as a "Dynasty."

These can be explained scientifically in terms of three [3] doctrinal positions: a] opposites or conflicting contraries, b] transmutation or the fluidity of change and, c] the functional life of the universe caused by "the Four [4] Elements": FIRE, WATER, EARTH, AIR.

1. See Yosef ben-Jochannan's BLACK MAN OF THE NILE AND HIS FAMILY, pages 130 - 164

These basically scientific and theosophic dimensions involved in the teachings and/or principles upon which all of the so-called JUDAEO-CHRISTIAN-ISLAMIC "sects" are based p dated Thales and Socrates, muchless Plato and Aristotle. Yet, it was the latter so-called GR PHILOSOPHER whom European/American "academicians" gave credit for their origin. But, course the fact that neither of these so-called GREEK PHILOSOPHERS was in existence befor ca. 600 B.C.E., particularly Aristotle who supposedly became famous through his associatio with Alexander "the great" [the son of Phillip of Macedonia, or Macedon] conquest of Ta-Mer in ca. 332 B.C.E., means nothing. The most recent of the major academic distortions on thi point was shown on page 175 of the RUSICRUCIAN DIGEST, May 1952; its most pronounced as pect being the "ONE AND ONLY TRUE GOD" concept in the DEIFICATION of the Hebrew [Jew ish] God YWH, Christian God JESUS "the Christ," and Moslem God AL'LAH. There are many other Judaeo-Christian-Islamic "SECTS" and/or "OFFSHOOTS" that maintain this base.

If one choses to breakdown THE DIAGRAM OF THE LAW OF OPPOSITES into its relative religious [theosophical] understanding the following details become that much more necessary

1. The composition of one SQUARE within another SQUARE pinpoints the function of the ELEMENTS with the QUALITIES;
2. The establishment of the INNER SQUARE on the hypothenuse shows the relationship of a given ELEMENT to a QUALITY; and
3. The corners of the SQUARE show mid-point connections of the four RIGHT ANGLE TRIANGLES in the INNER as the four OUTER SEGMENTS.

What we are in fact dealing with here is nothing more than that which Socrates preferred change for his own convenience and call...

"THE DOCTRINE OF THE NOUS"....

The Hebrews, Christians and Moslems, to a great extent equally the Greeks of the Druid reli translated this into their VERSION of the THEOSOPHICAL TRANSMUTATION OF THE MIND the name "GOD". The DEITY [God] is either YWH, JESUS or AL'LAH, depending upon whose ligion of the three [3] so-called "WESTERN RELIGIONS [Judaism, Christianity and Islam]" G Head is at issue at the given time and place.

Here we can see that "MIND" and "INTELLIGENT CAUSATION" are equal to the "GOD" a "CREATION" Socrates supposedly analyzed as the original...

"SUMMUM BONUM" or "LAW OF THE GREATEST GOOD"....

I call upon William Turner's HISTORY OF PHILOSOPHY, page 82, Xenophon's MEMORABILI I, 2 and 4, Yosef ben-Jochannan's BLACK MAN OF THE NILE AND HIS FAMILY, pages 312 - 338, and AFRICA: MOTHER OF "WESTERN CIVILIZATION, pages 375 - 453, for further det ed evidence on the above facts and distortions.

Somewhat looking back, we must remember that even Pythagoras also claimed to have developed "A SYSTEM" that explained "THE TRANSMUTATION OF THE MIND", allegedly based upon The Doctrine Of a] OPPOSITES, b] SUMMUM BONUM or SUPREME GOOD and, c] PROCESS OF PURIFICATION.

In the case of item b] the HUMAN PERSON in MAN becomes as much "CHRIST" [or "ANOINTED"] as was the Christians' God-Head called "JESUS". Thus it is that so many believe that the TRANSMUTATION of his life became the TRANSMIGRATION of his soul; this being also the split difference of time between life and death - the PROCESS OF PURIFICATION that caused his DEIFICATION. For this reason those of us under Greek orientation and Judaeo/Christian theosophical thoughts must maintain that this original African teaching was not included within the basic roots of...

"THE UNION OF THE LAW OF OPPOSITES"....

Pythagoras of the Island of Samos, who was said to have been born about ca. 530 B.C.E., allegedly felt that this original AFRICAN DOCTRINE should be divided into three [3] parts:

i] TRANSMIGRATION, ii] IMMORTALITY OF THE SOUL and, iii] SALVATION.

Here is where the Judaeo-Christian-Islamic theology of LIFE/DEATH and BODY/SOUL concept of "SALVATION" takes hold of the basic THEORY that created the Nile Valley Africans' High-Cultures "DIAGRAM OF THE LAW OF OPPOSITES". The facts relative to this area of "GREEK PHILOSOPHY" are shown in Ruddick's HISTORY OF PHILOSOPHY, Fuller's HISTORY OF PHILOSOPHY, and Roger's STUDENTS'HISTORY OF PHILOSOPHY, pages 14 - 22; each under the similar subtitle - "The Life and Tenets of Pythagoras". John Kendrick's HISTORY OF ANCIENT EGYPT, Volume I, pages 401 - 402, and William Turner's HISTORY OF PHILOSOPHY, pages 40 - 43, are further supportive materials to be used in your own investigation of the facts.

We have arrived at the critical point where our own original African/Asian Judaic, Judaeo-Christian and Islamic "ONE AND ONLY TRUE GOD" [deity] in the invisible personality of YWH, JESUS "the Christ", and/or AL'LAH theory generally takes leave of our ability to rationalize beyond the point of saying that other peoples' God and Religion are:

"PAGANISM" and/or "HEATHENISM".

The "Paganism/Heathenism" in this issue was brought about by the THEORY and TEACHING we find in the BEGINNING OF THE WORLD and ORIGIN OF MAN propagandized in the Hebrew [on Israelite] and Christian FIRST BOOK OF MOSES [Genesis] of the FIVE BOOKS OF MOSES [Holy Torah, Comesh, Old Testament, etc.]. Yet we can, or should, clearly observe that the ancient and/or modern writers and scribes who wrote the DIFFERENT VERSIONS of this STORY could not distinguish between GOD'S intent to deal with an ALL-PERFECT HUMAN RACE He CREATED and ordered to...

BE FRUITFUL, AND MULTIPLY, AND REPLENISH THE EARTH, AND SUBDUE IT: AND HAVE DOMINION OVER THE FISH OF THE SEA, AND OVER THE FOWL OF THE AIR, AND OVER EVERY LIVING THING THAT MOVETH UPON THE EARTH...,

etc. according to GENESIS i : 28. Yet all of the allegorical and mythological background mater als and philosophical inputs in this VERSION relative to the CREATION OF MAN AND WOMAN [the human race] reveal a distinct contradiction in the second story about "The Beginning Of Tl World"; thus:

AND THE LORD GOD FORMED MAN OF THE DUST OF THE GROUND, AND BREATHED INTO HIS NOSTRILS THE BREATH OF LIFE; AND MAN BECAME A LIVING SOUL,

according to GENESIS ii : 7. WOMAN in this latter story was not in the picture, as shown in th first one above, until GOD [Jehovah, Jesus "the Christ"[1] or Al'lah] had second thoughts in anot section of "His Holy Scriptures" - GENESIS ii : 21 - 23:

AND THE LORD GOD CAUSED A DEEP SLEEP TO FALL UPON ADAM, AND HE SLEPT: AND HE TOOK ONE OF HIS RIBS, AND CLOSED UP THE FLESH INSTEAD THEREOF;

AND THE RIB WHICH THE LORD GOD HAD TAKEN FROM MAN HE MADE A WOMAN, AND BROUGHT HER UNTO THE MAN.

AND MAN SAID, "THIS IS NOW BONE OF MY BONES, AND FLESH OF MY FLESH: SHE SHALL BE CALLED WOMAN, BECAUSE SHE WAS TAKEN OUT OF MAN".

You will notice that all of the above stories and VERSIONS are merely off-shoots from h dreds, maybe thousands, of other much more ancient works that predated the first HEBREW o ISRAELITE diviner and/or allegorist; even before the first man - AVRAM or ABRAHAM - to h proclaimed a new "GOD" named "YWH" [Jehovah, etc.] during his lifetime in the City of UR o Kingdom of Chaldea,near the area where the Tigris and Euphrates rivers make their tangential connection north of the beginning of the Gulf of Persia [Iran] that empty's its waters into the In [Indian] Ocean. To understand all of what I have just revealed here requires your very careful examination of the following works I have previously introduced to you in other lectures,and at library in my home when you made your FIELD TRIP in October of this year - 1974 C.E.:

BOOK OF THE COMING FORTH BY DAY AND BY NIGHT [or Egyptian Book Of The Dead], PAPYRUS OF ANI, PYRAMID TEXTS, COFFIN TEXTS, OSIRIAN DRAMA, EDWIN C. SMITH PAPYRUS, TEACHINGS OF PHARAOH AMEN-EM-EOPE, TEACHINGS OF PHARAOH AKHENATON [Amenhotep IVth, Amorphis Ivth, etc.], NEGATIVE CONFESSIONS, THE GODS OF EGYPT, WRITINGS OF QUEEN/KING HAT-SHEP-SUT,...etc.

Added to the above works must be included certain writers who lived and wrote their works in attempt at clarifying the ancient teachings of the indigenous [BLACK] Africans at a period whe the African SCRIPT we call "HIEROGLYPHICS" today were only knowledgable to a very closel guarded and selectively secret few; such as:

> G. Higgins' ANACALYSIS [2 vols.], J. Frazer's THE GOLDEN BOUGH [13 vols.], G. Maspero's HISTORY OF EGYPT [8 vols], THE DAWN OF CIVILIZATION, G. Massey's EGYPT THE LIGHT OF THE WORLD [2 vols.], BOOK OF THE BEGINNINGS [2 vols.], A. Churchward's SIGNS AND SYMBOLS OF PRIMORDIAL MAN, G.G.M. James' STOLEN LEGACY, H. Frankfort's HISTORY OF PHILOSOPHY, S. Clymer's FIRE PHILOSOPHY, J. G. Jackson's GOD, MAN AND CIVILIZATION.

Along with all of the works shown above, you are to add those used in this text and the work-book assigned this class, ben-Jochannan's BLACK MAN OF THE NILE AND HIS FAMILY, as aids. Of course the following information will equally add to your bibliography, but only in context to your understanding of the constant researches you will have to make in libraries and other depositories containing millions of artifacts, papyri, scrolls, books, etc., etc., etc. stolen from the indigenous African [BLACK] People by their [OUR] European, European-American and Asian conquerors, slavers and colonizers who began their plundering of Alkebu-lan [AFRICA] and her sons and daughters [so-called "BANTUS, BLACK AFRICANS, AFRICANS SOUTH OF THE SAHARA," etc.] when the Hyksos ["SHEPHERD KINGS OF BEDUINA"] conquered the delta area of Ta-Merry [EGYPT] around ca. 1675 B.C.E. [the XIVth Dynasty]. Yet, it was from the reign [rule] of the Macedonian-Greeks with Alexander "the great" in ca. 332 B.C.E. and General Soter [renamed Ptolemy Ist, in what is being called the "XXXth DYNASTY" by European and European-American academicians to date], along with the Romans who came in ca. 47 or 30 B.C.E., that the RAPING of Ta-Merry and the rest of North Alkebu-lan up to the present Arab descendants - whose ancestors arrived in ca 640 C.E. or A.D. [18 A.H.], we must hold responsible.[1] However, as you try to piece together the ancient history and cultural heritage of the indigenous African People, particularly those of the Nile Valley, North, Northeast, Northwest and East Alkebu-lan, and find that most of the available documents are in Europe, European-America and Asia, but not in Alkebu-lan, you will see that much more significance in the following as you realize that all of the acts of CULTURAL GENOCIDE directed against the Africans, even today, had to be done in order to maintain the Judaeo-Christian-Islamic myths and allegories related to the "ONE AND ONLY TRUE GOD" religious teachings and the "DEMOCRATIC" theology that allegedly originated from the so-called "GREEK PHILOSOPHERS".

THE DENUDING OF ALKEBU-LAN [Africa] AND HER INDIGENOUS PEOPLE'S, ETC.

We can begin with Emperor Theodosius, who issued the first "EDICT" that started the final downfall of the teachings of the MYSTERIES from the Nile Valley High-Cultures up to the Fourth Century C.E. For up to this period of earliest European-style Christianity in Rome and Greece

1. See Yosef ben-Jochannan's BLACK MAN OF THE NILE AND HIS FAMILY, pages 251 - 271.

the Mysteries System's SECRETS were taught unabated throughout all of Roman and Greek Eu Thus it was that Emperor Theodosius, whose order that the OSIRIAN LODGES and TEMPLES closed and sealed, and that all AFRICAN [Egyptian, Nubian, Meröite, Itiopian, Puanit, etc.] DIVINITIES, including the HERCULEAN WORSHIP OF ISIS[1] and HER SON OSIRIS in Rome, b suppressed, proved to have been the main blow of the destruction of African PHILOSOPHY, T OSOPHY and THEOLOGY in all of Europe that lasted until the present day. And due to him, we are still unable to observe said values in the Judaeo-Christian BIBLES in use today; particula those in which the PURE [sterile] LILY WHITE GOD, HEAVEN and ANGELS appear in picture lustrations by European and European-American editors and censors - like the example below

A SCENE FROM THE HERCULANEUM WORSHIP OF ISIS. This form of worship of the first Virgin Mother was common among the ancient Greeks and Romans in Greece and Rome for hundreds of years before, and up to, the adoption of "African Christianity" by the Roman Emperor Constantine "the great" in ca. 312 C.E. upon his rise to the throne. [From a fresco dating back to the pre-Christian Era in Rome]

How can WE relate and translate what WE are doing here at AFRICANA STUDIES and RESEARCH CENTER to the above experience of the indigenous African [BLACK] People and thei European [WHITE] People understudies in terms of this and other courses taught by other professors? Can WE interpret the above and relate it to the infamous SLAVE TRADE and DEMOG RAPHY of Alkebu-lan by the SLAVERS from Asia, Europe and European-America, beginning f ca. 640 C.E. [or 18 A.H.] to ca. 1865 C.E. [or 1243 A.H.]? Can WE relate the suppression o the African religion of the WORSHIP OF THE GOD OSIRIS AND GODESS ISIS and the SLAVE

1. See Yosef ben-Jochannn's THE BLACK MAN'S RELIGION, pages 64 - 69 [Volume III].

TRADE to the colonial experience that culminated in the "PARTITION OF AFRICA" [Alkebu-lan] and the BERLIN CONFERENCE and BRUSSELS CONFERENCE of ca. 1884 - 1885 and 1886 - 1896 C.E. in Berlin, Germany and Brussels, Belgium? Give an oral demonstration to the class.

We can use Max Muller's EGYPTIAN MYTHOLOGY, pages 241 - 243 and Y. ben-Jochannan's THE BLACK MAN'S RELIGION, Vol. III, etc. with respect to the HERCULEAN WORSHIP OF ISIS, Henry Nevinson's A MODERN SLAVERY and E.D. Morel's THE BLACK MAN'S BURDEN with respect to SLAVERY and the SLAVE TRADE; and Sir Edward Hertslett's THE MAP OF AFRICA BY TREATY, Vol. II, Sir J. Scott-Keltie's THE PARTITION OF AFRICA and THE BERLIN CONFERENCE with respect to ASIAN and EUROPEAN-AMERICAN IMPERIALISM and COLONIALISM in Alkebu-lan.

As we return to the DESTRUCTION OF AFRICAN RELIGIOUSITY and PHILOSOPHY in ancient Rome/Greece we are forced to recognize that it was Emperor Theodosius' EDICT of the Fourth Century C.E. in consort with the hierarchy of the Roman Catholic Christian Church, along with disasterous effect of stopping all of the indigenous African teachings of the MYSTERIES SYSTEM from the GRAND LODGE OF LUXOR [located on the banks of the Nile River] that were still being practiced by the indigenous Africans called "MOBADIANS" and "BLEMMIANS", who lived on the Island of Philae and along the banks of the Nile River at the First Cataract [as shown on the map on the following page]:

SUBORDINATE LODGES OF THE GRAND LODGE OF LUXOR [1]

1. Palestiue [at Mt. Carmel]	10. Rhodes
2. Assyria [at Mt. Herman in Lebanon]	11. Delphi
3. Babylon	12. Miletus
4. Media [near the Red Sea]	13. Cyprus
5. India [at the banks of the Ganges River]	14. Corinth
6. Burma	15. Crete
7. Athens	16. Cush [Itiopi, Ethiopia]
8. Rome [at Elea]	17. Monomotapa [South Africa]
9. Croton	18. Zimbabwe [Rhodesia]

LUXOR was destroyed by fire, burnt to the ground, in the year c. 548 B.C.E. It was set aflame by foreigners who were jealous of the indigenous Africans ["Negroes,"et al] knowledge of the "MYSTERIES" taught in the Osirica - which included all of the above mentioned disciplines. [See John Kendrick's, ANCIENT EGYPT, Book II, p. 363; Eva B. Sandford's, THE MEDITERRANEAN WORLD, pp. 135 - 139; Yosef ben-Jochannan's, AFRICA: MOTHER OF "WESTERN CIVILIZATION", Chapter IX].

The African teachers we are dealing with were suppressed because they dared to reject the Roman [or European] distorters "CHRISTIAN DOCTRINES" that converted ISIS to MARY and OSIRIS to JOSEPH or the God-Head YWH [Jehovah], all of which had been edited to the point that it could no longer be recognize from its African origin when African "Israelites [Hebrews] of

1. See Yosef ben-Jochannan's BLACK MAN OF THE NILE AND HIS FAMILY, pages 251 - 254.

[Note that Europe was not yet in history]

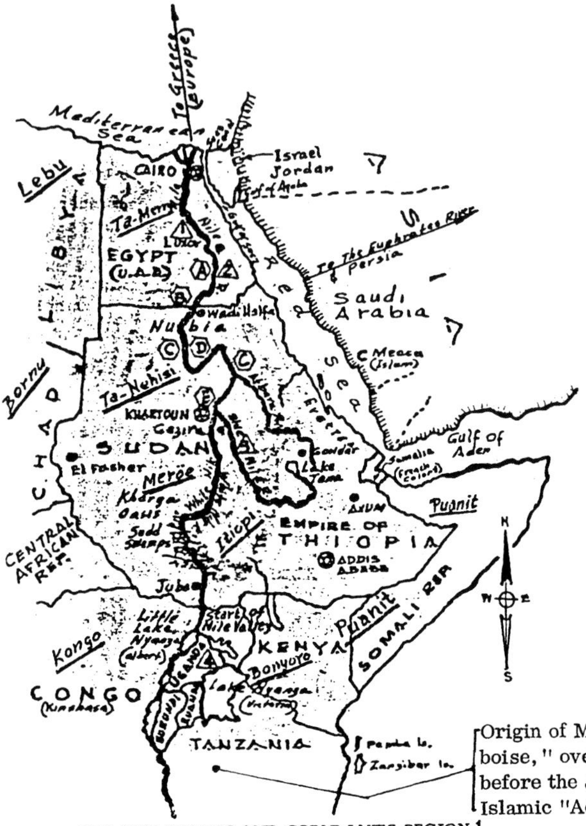

Origin of MAN, "Zinjanthropus boise," over 1.7 million years before the Judaeo-Christian-Islamic "Adam" only 5735 years.

THE NILE VALLEYS AND GREAT LAKES REGION [1]

ca. 4100 BCE - 1975 C.E. [A.D.]

KEY

Cataracts: A, B, and C
Dams: ⚠1 Asiut ⚠2 Aswan ⚠3 Sennar
⚠4 Nyanza (Owens) Falls
[4,100 + statute miles, south to north]

Ta-Merry [Egypt] wrote the first "CHRISTIAN SCRIPTURES" in ca. 50 - 100 C.E. we now cal the "KOINÊ BIBLE or NEW TESTAMENT.

Emperor Justinian's second EDICT in the Sixth Century C.E. made the indigenous Africar

1. See Yosef ben-Jochannan's BLACK MAN OF THE NILE AND HIS FAMILY, Chapter IV. The map above tells the story why the Black Man ["Negro"] must be removed from Nile Valley hist

n Ta-Nehisi [Zeti, Nubia, Sudan, etc.] who had from centuries before maintained their teachngs about, and worship of, Nile Valley and Great Lakes "DIVINITIES" [Gods and/or Godesses] rop their public allegiance to same, but instead outwardly proclaim their loyalty to the NEW :ELIGION [Christianity] and its God-Head JESUS "the Christ" [the Annointed]. In the meantime ıe PRIESTS of the MYSTERIES SYSTEM in Ta-Merry, Ta-Nehisi, Meröe and other nations of orth and Northeast Alkebu-lan began dying-off; and not a single young man was allowed to be rained to replace them. The SCRIBES were prohibited from writing in any language not familiar ɔ the Roman officials both in the government and the OFFICIAL RELIGION - Roman Catholic hristianity. Thus was the beginning of the end to HIEROGLYPHIC SCRIPTS of any kind, particurly those relative to the teachings about the GOD and GODESSES. The first aspect of this probition was to change the origin of the WORSHIP OF THE VIRGIN MOTHER AND CHILD or GODSS ISIS AND HER CHILD HORUS as the original IMMACULATE CONCEPTION and/or VIRGIN IRTH the Romans attributed to MARY AND THE JESUS CHILD. It must be remembered that the ame BLACK MADONNA AND CHILD was still retained for Mary and Jesus as it had been used r Isis and Horus even after Michaelangelo was commissioned by Pope Julius IVth to paint the soalled "HOLY FAMILY" [Joseph, Mary and Jesus] on the ceiling of the Cistene Chaple of Saint eter's Basilica in Rome, Italy, which he completed in ca. 1511 C.E. [see Y. ben-Jochannan's HE BLACK MAN'S RELIGION, Vol. II].[1] You will notice that this conduct by the church and tate was part and parcel of the military role and colonial partition of Alkebu-lan started by mperor Constantine ["the great"] and continued by Emperor Theodosius and Justinian, along ith all of the others between them. The suppression of the Osirica's MYSTERIES SYSTEM with s GRAND LODGE on the banks of the Nile River and SUBORDINATE LODGES throughout Asia ıd Europe was never eased up until the latter half of the Eighteenth Century C.E. when the rench [European] colonial and imperial occupation of Ta-Merry [Egypt, Sais, Qamt, Mizrain, :c.] also resulted in the RAPE of the indigenous African [BLACK] People's artifacts, such as e world famous "ROSETTA STONE" we see on the following page of this pamphlet, and which detailed in Y. ben-Jochannan's BLACK MAN OF THE NILE AND HIS FAMILY, pages 280 - 282 ıd COLLECTIVE THOUGHTS OF THE PHILOSOPHY OF A BLACK HISTORIAN TODAY [an unblished manuscript], pages 1 - 20.

The religion and theology created and developed by the indigenous Africans that eventually anched off into Greece and Rome as the "OSIRIAN CYCLE", and later called by so-called "conrvative" and "liberal" White egyptologists "GRECO-EGYPTIAN SERAPIS', with its Nile Valley se culture had began its final path to destruction. The oblisks, sphinxes and temples built by

See Y. ben-Jochannan's AFRICAN ORIGIN OF THE MAJOR "WESTERN RELIGIONS", Chapt. II

GRAPHIC REPRODUCTION OF THE "ROSETTA STONE" [1]

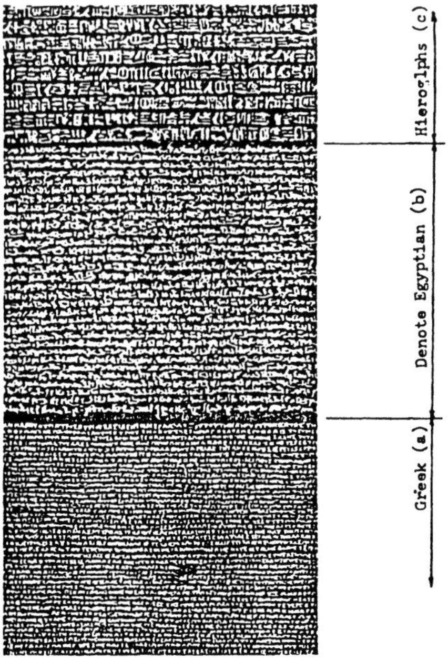

The "Rosetta Stone" was illegally taken from Egypt by one of Napoleon's army officers in 1799 C.E. during the French invasion of Egypt, Africa. It is presently located in the British Museum, London, England.

The inscriptions on the stone are divided into three different languages:
a) The lowest layer of the writings is in Greek.
b) The middle layer of the writings is in a Demotic Script.
c) The top layer of the writings is in Hieroglyphic (Egyptian).

In 1822 Jean Champollion, a Frenchman with an extensive knowledge of Greek, was able to read the lowest layer of the stone and compared it with the other two layers, thereby breaking the "mystery" of the language used in Egypt, North Africa, in which most of the history we know about ancient Egypt is written. This foundation laid the groundwork for what is today called "Egyptology" (the study of the ancient civilizations of Egypt).

the indigenous Africans from the Nile Valley and Great Lakes regions of Alkebu-lan and transferred to Europe in conjunction of the WORSHIP OF ISIS AND OSIRIS were desecrated by the officials of the Roman Catholic Christian Church and Religion. They even ordered that the top each and every obelisk and stela in Rome must have affixed to it a "CROSS" or "CRUCIFIX" to give the impression that they were the works of the "Christians". The vast majority of these R

1. See Yosef ben-Jochannan's BLACK MAN OF THE NILE AND HIS FAMILY, pages 277 - 282.

ıans were even made to believe that these stolen obelisks and stalae from Ta-Nehisi and Ta-Ierry were designed and built by their fellow Europeans of Greece and/or Rome [particularly 'hristians]. Yet, the further production of said artifacts were prohibited. They went further by ssuing other EDICTS that suppressed the rituals which still taught that the NILE VALLEY was ne only "HOLY LAND" and/or "PROMISE [Promisedland] LAND". [1]

One should easily understand that the suppression of the WORSHIP OF ISIS AND HORUS as 'IRGIN MOTHER AND CHILD was solely to make way for the WORSHIP OF MARY AND JESUS as ne new VIRGIN MOTHER AND CHILD a-la-European [Roman in this case] style. But, in neither ase of the two situations was the MALE FIGURE [Horus and Joseph] given recognition of having nything whatever to do with the procreation of the GOD-HEAD Osiris and/or Christ. Yet Joseph as an active and actual HUMAN PERSON who lived amongst other Israelites [Hebrews or Jews], nd witnesses his woman [MARY] carrying a baby in her WOMB that was supposedly placed there Y AN ANGEL OF THE LORD; whereas HORUS was his own FICTIONAL FATHER, who was also alled OSIRIS in his celestial and cosmic state of being - never an ACTUAL HUMAN PERSON. ote very carefully that HORUS became OSIRIS following his own DEATH and DEIFICATION - the tter following his RESURRECTION. On the otherhand JESUS became "THE CHRIST" and/or the OLY GHOST[2] following His own DEATH, RESURRECTION and DEIFICATION. Here you can see at it was obvious these GODS - Osiris and the Christ - could not exist symultaneously with the essings of the ruling officials of the Roman Catholic Christian Church; particularly when it had lready become the most powerful religious group because of its military and colonialist plunder-g and raping of Europe, Asia and Alkebu-lan by Emperor Constantine ["the great"] under the anner of CHRISTIANITY and its God-Head JESUS "the Christ" [Annointed], all of which was sup-orted and carried forward by Emperor Theodosius and Emperor Justinian, Popes included.

Strange as it was, the Romans dared not proclaim ROME the "HOLY LAND". The people ere already conditioned to understand and believe that Alkebu-lan and Asia produced the WOR-HIP OF OSIRIS and JESUS "the Christ". For it was to Alkebu-lan and Asia that most of their oted SCRIBES and PRIESTS went to study and receive their "AUTHORITY" and/or "RECOGNI-ION" in the "PRIESTHOOD OF THE OSIRICA'S MYSTERIES SYSTEM", and to become register-l at the Osirisa's GRAND LODGE located on the bank of the Nile River. In otherwords, it was ong the Nile River Valley that the first European "CHRISTIANS" came to "PAY HOMAGE" as eir PROMISE LAND and/or HOLY LAND. The removal of Ta-Merrian, Ta-Nihisian, Itiopian d Puanit names and their replacement by others from Greece and Rome attached to the teachings the OSIRICA'S WORSHIP OF ISIS AND OSIRIS also added to the de-Africanization of all of North

See Y. ben-Jochannan's WE THE BLACK JEWS: WITNESS TO THE JEWISH RACE MYTH.
The term "Holy Spirit" is a modern refine of the original "Holy Ghost" Christians used.

Alkebu-lan and Nile Valley religious teachings and divinities, and of course made them part their Europeanized VERSIONS, all of which amounted to the beginning of CULTURAL GENOC against the indigenous African [BLACK] People and their original works.

I am moved to ask that you also read pages 141 - 153 of Sedgwick and Tyler's HISTORY SCIENCE,along with page 31 of the "Introduction" in Zeller's HISTORY OF PHILOSOPHY,wit gards to how the OSIRICA'S TEACHINGS and WORSHIP spread all over southern Europe and western Asia from North and Northeast Alkebu-lan [Africa] and became known as the TEACH OF SOPHIA by the Greeks and Romans. In this latter context the added works of Max Muller' EGYPTIAN MYTHOLOGY, George G.M. James' STOLEN LEGACY, Eva Sandford's THE ME TERRANEAN WORLD, Count C.F. Volney's RUINS OF EMPIRE, and Gaston Maspero's HIST OF EGYPT [8 vols.] should be of greatest importance.

The ORIGINAL TEACHINGS of the OSIRICA by the indigenous Africans of the Nile Valley Great Lakes High-Cultures - now translated, edited and perverted into what is being called t "JUDAISM, CHRISTIANITY, JUDAEO-CHRISTIANITY, ISLAM",[1] etc.- that produced all the called "SACRED SCRIPTURES WRITTEN BY GOD-INSPIRED HOLY SCRIBES". But, the orig sources from whence these so-called Judaeo-Christian-Islamic SCRIPTURES had their birth now relegated to the obscurity of "SECT, HEATHENISM, IDOLATRY, SATANISM", etc., etc etc.; and of course the descendants of the indigenous African [BLACK] People who created an developed them are equally relegated to obscurity. Yet, I must remind you of the following fr Count C.F. Volney's RUINS OF EMPIRE, page xii of the "Introduction", written in 1792 C.E

> THERE A PEOPLE NOW FORGOTTEN DISCOVERED WHILE OTHERS WERE YET BARBARIANS, THE ELEMENTS OF THE ARTS AND SCIENCES. A RACE OF MEN NOW REJECTED FOR THEIR SABLE SKIN AND FRIZZLED HAIR, FOUNDED ON THE STUDY ON THE LAWS OF NATURE THOSE CIVIL AND RELIGIOUS SYSTEMS WHICH STILL GOVERN THE UNIVERSE.

All of the SECTS, HEATHENISMS, IDOLATRIES and SATANISMS are still visible in the HOLY and GOD-INSPIRED SACRED SCRIBES'most noted SACRED SCRIPTURES under the la of PENTATEUCH [Five Books Of Moses, Holy Torah, Old Testament, etc.], KOINÊ BIBLE [Testament] and QUR'AN [Holy Koran].[3] Yet, we are to find that the indigenous African who ma all three [3] of these so-called "WESTERN RELIGIONS" - Judaism, Christianity and Islam eq meaningful on the face of the globe - MOSHE or MOSES - was born in Ta-Merry along with al his people bearing the name "ISRAELITES" and/or "HARIBU [Jews]". Note that Ta-Merry, e

---

1. See PENTATEUCH [Old Testament or Holy Torah], KOINÊ BIBLE [New Testament] and H QUR'AN [Koran].

2. The name "Christian" was not in use until the Council Of Antioch. Jesus Christ means Jos "the anointed"; "Christ" or "Crystos" having derived its origin from ancient Greek.

3. All three have coopted teachings from the Africans' BOOK OF THE DEAD another works.

ly Ta-Nehisi, Itiopi, Meröe and Puanit were also indigenous African [BLACK] nations[1] that existed for thousands of years before there was an "ADAM AND EVE" mentioned anywhere in prehistory and/or history; and that all of these nations appeared as shown on the map below:

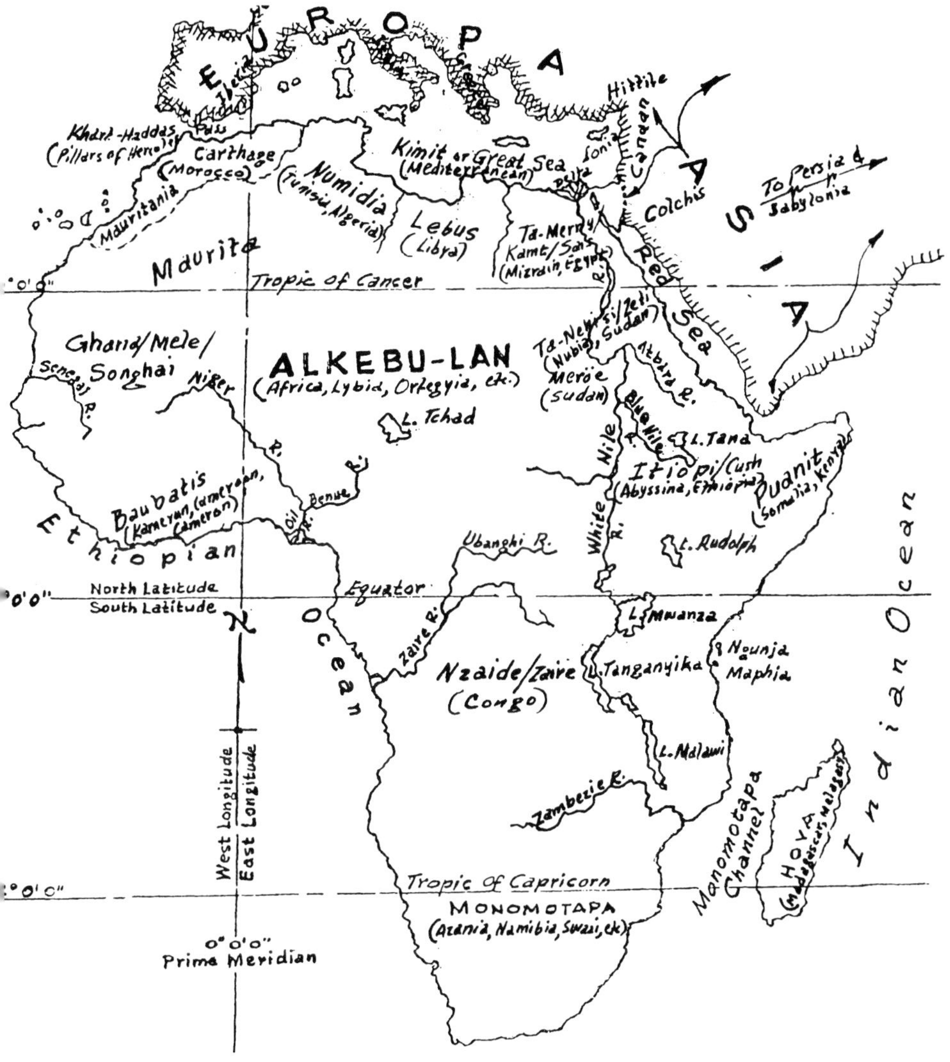

A MAP OF ALKEBU-LAN AND SURROUNDING CONTINENTS
[Approximately ca. 1236 B.C.E. Greece and/or Rome was not yet in History until 600 B.C.E.]

1. See texts by Chancellor Williams and Cheikh Anta Diop along with Yosef ben-Jochannan's.

Added to the MAP OF ALKEBU-LAN on the previous page are the indigenous nations of t African People we call "MARITANIANS" and/or "KHART-HADDANS", who were also known a "CARTHAGENIANS" and "MOORS" during earlier and later periods both Before The Christia Era [B.C.E or B.C.] and During The Christian Era [C.E. or A.D.]. I have carefully left out the map the following places - waterways, oceans, seas, etc. which you are to locate in their geographical perspective:

OCEANUS AETIOPICUS, NUMIDIA, LEBUS, MAURITUS, GREAT or KIMIT SEA, RED SEA, MOUNT HOREB or MOUNT SINAI, INDUS OCEAN, PUANIT, GREAT LAKES, FOUR OTHER NAMES BY WHICH ALKEBU-LAN WAS KNOWN TO THE ANCIENTS DURING THE PERIOD OF ca. 500 B. C. E. AND LATER.

MAP
Of AFRICA[1]
1688 C.E.

AFRICA, by the Ancients, was called Olympia, Hesperia, Oceania, Coryphe, Ammonis, Ortygia, and Ethiopia. By the Greeks and Romans, Lybis and Africa. By the Aethiopians and Moors, Alkebu-lan.

Note: The European colonialists, from the 15th through 19th Century, C.E. refused to accept their ignorance of "AFRICA'S" interior and made all sorts of MAPS with waterways, mountains, nations and peoples which did not exist on the continent.

1. Note that the current MAP OF "AFRICA" was divided at the Berlin and Brussels conferenc of ca. 1884 - 1885 and ca. 1886 - 1896 C.E. following the "PARTITION OF AFRICA" by Europeans and European-Americans [see Sir Edward Hertslett's MAP OF AFRICA BY TREATY, London, 1895, Volume II of III]. Many of the above names of nations, rivers and other waterwa places, etc. are on this map; all appears on the map on page 15 - placed there by the Students

REQUIREMENTS FOR THE "FINAL PAPER", ETC. DUE DEC. 13, 1974

Use The Following BIBLIOGRAPHY On Pages 18 - 21 For Documenting The Final Paper.

1. Document the entire ESSAY with AFRICAN sources only.
2. Document the entire ESSAY with ASIAN sources only.
3. Document the entire ESSAY with EUROPEAN and EUROPEAN-AMERICAN sources only.
4. Using your own words and method of presentation [according to the standard established at AFRICANA STUDIES and RESEARCH CENTER for MASTER'S DEGREE candidates] and extend this ESSAY at least FIVE more typwritten pages - double spaced.
5. Pinpoint in the following author's works...

    G. Higgins' ANACALYPSIS [2 Volumes]
    G. Massey's EGYPT THE LIGHT OF THE WORLD [2 Volumes]
    G.G.M. James' STOLEN LEGACY
    J. Frazer's THE GOLDEN BOUGH [13 Volumes]
    G. Maspero's A HISTORY OF EGYPT [8 Volumes]
    J.H. Breastead's ANCIENT RECORDS OF ANCIENT EGYPT [5 Volumes]
    C.F. Volney's RUINS OF EMPIRE
    V. Denon's TRAVELS IN EGYPT AND ASSYRIA
    E.A.W. Budge's [ed./transl.] EGYPTIAN BOOK OF THE DEAD
    E.A.W. Budge's [ed./transl.] PAPYRUS OF ANI
    THE PENTATEUCH [Holy Torah, Comesh, Old Testament, etc.; any Version]
    THE KOINÊ BIBLE [New Testament, etc.; and Version]
    THE HOLY QUR'AN [Koran, etc.; any Version]
    G. Maspero's THE DAWN OF CIVILIZATION [8 Volumes]
    H.W. Smith's MAN AND HIS GODS...

    the statement and/or statements that tied so-called "WESTERN CIVILIZATION" to its "AFRICAN [Black] ORIGIN", as explained both by Count C. F. Volney's RUINS OF EMPIRE he wrote in ca. 1792 C.E., and that of Sir G. Higgins' ANACALYPSIS he wrote in ca. 1848 C.E. [or A.D.].

6. Analyze, and write a critical analysis of this ESSAY from the perspective of an African HISTORIAN, using the skills and resources you have acquired here at AFRICANA STUDIES and RESEARCH CENTER'S LIBRARY. You may use information of an original nature, providing same has been carefully documented in your "FINAL PAPER".

Note:The following "FINAL PAPERS" on pages 22 - 45 by the Students [Co-Authors] were written after the completion of each and everyone of the first FIVE [5] REQUIREMENTS above. The SIXTH [6th] is the "FINAL PAPERS" you are about to read. Equally note that there were other reading assignments, and a "FIELD TRIP" to the Museum of Natural History [New York, N.Y.] to examine original artifacts pertinent to "Africa's" antiquity, also to Prof. ben-Jochannan's LIBRARY of very specialized books and maps of Alkebu-lan ["Africa"]. All of this spread over the entire Fall Semester's work. Give special attention to item No. 4 above; for the Students' "FINAL PAPERS" are to reflect this DIRECTIVE more so than anything else. This is the juncture where one can truly observe the kind of INDEPENDENT THINKERS the Faculty of Africana Studies and Research Center develops year after year; hopefully an indication of BLACK/ AFRICAN STUDIES everywhere else [Yosef ben-Jochannan, Visiting Professor of History].

EXTENDED BIBLIOGRAPHY FOR THIS PAMPHLET: by Y. ben-Jochannan.

General

Botsford, G. W., "A History of the Ancient World, New York, 1911

Breasted, J. H., "Ancient Times," New York, 1935

Bury, J. B., S. A. Cook, F. E. Adcock, and M. P. Charlesworth, "Cambridge Ancient History, 12 Vols., 5 Vols. of plates, New York, 1923.

Bury, J. B., "A History of Greece to the Death of Alexander the Great," London, 1951

Hall, H. R. H., "Ancient History of the Near East, 9th ed., London, 1936

Marrou, H. I., "A History of Education in Antiquity," New York, 1956

Newbigin, M. A., "The Mediterranean Lands," London, 1924

Rostortzeff, M. A., "A History of the Ancient World (transl. by J. D. Duff) 2 Vols. 2nd ed., Oxford, 1933

Sandys, J. E., "History of Classical Scholarship" 2 Vols. 3rd ed., New York, 1921

Starr, G. G., "A History of the Ancient World," New York, 1965

Thomson, J. G., "History of Ancient Geography, Cambridge, 1948

Ullman, B. L., "Ancient Writing and Its Influence," New York, 1932

Prehistory

Braidwood, R. J., "Prehistoric Men," Chicago, 1948

Burkitt, M. C., "The Old Stone Age." 2nd. ed., New York, 1949

Childe, V. G., "The Dawn of European Civilization," 4th ed., New York, 1948

------, "New Light on the Most Ancient East," New York, 1934

------, "What Happened in History," Hammondsworth, 1948

Coon, C. S., "The Origin of Races," New York, 1962

-----, "The Races of Europe," New York, 1939

Hooton, E. A., "Up from the Ape." Rev. ed., New York, 1946.

Houalls, W., "Mankind so Far," New York, 1945

Radin, P., "Primitive Religion," New York, 1937

Raphael, M., "Prehistoric Cave Paintings." (transl. by N. Guterman), New York, 1946

Vendryes, J., "Language, A Linguistic Introduction to History," (transl. by P. Radin), New York, 1931

Weidenrich, F., "Apes, Giants and Men," Chicago, 1946

Philosophy and Religion

Frankfort, H., "Kingship and the Gods." Chicago, 1948

Frankfort, H. et al, "Before Philosophy," New York, 1949

--------, "Intellectual Adventure of Ancient Man," Chicago, 1946

Gadd, C. J., "History and Monuments of Ur," New York, 1929

Egypt and the Nile

Alfred, C., "Old Kingdom Art in Ancient Egypt, London, 1946

[Bibliography continued]

Breasted, J. H., "Ancient Records of Egypt." 5 Vols., Chicago, 1906—07

--------, "A History of Egypt," 2nd ed., New York, 1935

Clarke, S. and R. Englebach, "Ancient Egyptian Masonry," Oxford, 1930

Drioton, E. and J. P. Lauer, "Sakkarah," Cairo, 1939

Edwards, I. E. S., "The Pyramids of Egypt," New York, 1947

Engleback, R., "Introduction to Egyptian Archaeology with special Reference to the Egyptian Museum, Cairo," Cairo, 1946

Erman, A., "The Literature of the Ancient Egyptians," (transl. by A. M. Blackman) London, 1927

Gardiner, A. H., "The Attitudes of the Ancient Egyptians to Death and the Dead," Cambridge, 1935

Glanville, S. R. K., "The Egyptians," London, 1933

--------, "Daily Life in Ancient Egypt," London, 1930

Peet, T. E., "A Comparative Study of the Literature of Egypt, Palestine, and Mesopotama," London, 1931

Pendleburry, J. D., "Tell-el-amarna," London, 1935

Petrie, W. M. F., "Seventy Years in Archaeology," New York, 1932

-----, "Arts and Crafts of Ancient Egypt," 2nd ed., London, 1910

Shorter, A. W., "An Introduction to Egyptian Religion," New York, 1939

------, "The Egyptian Gods," London, 1937

Winlock, H. E., "The Rise and Fall of the Middle Kingdom in Thebes," New York, 1947

Bell, H. I., "Egypt from Alexander to the Arab Conquest," Oxford, 1948

The Middle-East (Asia Minor)

Albright, W. F., "The Archaeology of Palestine," London, 1949

Bertholet, A., "A History of Hebrew Civilization," (transl. by A. K. Dallas), London, 1926

Bevan, E. R. and C. Singer (editors), "The Legacy of Israel," Oxford, 1927

Delaporte, L., "Los Hittites," Paris, 1936

Diringer, D., "The Alphabet," New York, 1948

Finegan, J., "Light from the Ancient Past," Princeton, 1946

Gurney, O. R., "The Hittites," Harmondsworth, 1964

Meek, T. J., "Hebrew Origins," New York, 1936

Moore, G. F., "History of Religions," 2 Vols., New York, 1937

Mendelsohn, I., "Slavery in the Ancient Near East," New York, 1949

Olmstead, A. T., "A History of the Persian Empire," Chicago, 1948

Rogers, R. W., "A History of Ancient Persia," New York, 1929

Sykes, P. M., "A History of Persia," 2 Vols, 3rd ed., London, 1930

North of the Mediterranean

Glotz, G., "The Aegean Civilization," (transl. by M. R. Dobie and E. M. Riley), New York, 1927

[Bibliography continued]

Hall, H. R., "The Civilization of Greece in the Bronze Age." London, 1928

Hutchinson, R. W., "Prehistoric Crete," Baltimore, 1963

Huxley, G. L., "Achaeans and Hittites," Oxford, 1960

------, "Crete and the Luwians," Oxford, 1961

Myres, J. L., "Who Were the Greeks?" Berkeley, 1930

Nilsson, M. P., "Homer and Mycenae," London, 1933

Page, D., "History and the Homeric Illiad," Berkeley, 1959

Person, A. W., "The Religion of Greece in Prehistoric Times," Berkeley, 1942

Starr, C. G., "The Origins of Greek Civilization," New York, 1961

Thomson, G., "Studies in Ancient Greek Society: The Prehistoric Agean," London, 1949

Young, A. M., "Troy and Her Legend," Pittsburgh, 1948

Botsford, G. W. and E. G. Sihler, "Hellenic Civilization," New York, 1920

Gary, M., "The Documentary Sources of Greek History," Oxford, 1927

Ferguson, W. S., "Greek Imperialism," New York, 1913

Grote, G., "A History of Greece," New ed. 12 vols., New York, 1906

Albright, W. F., "The Archaeology of Palestine," London, 1949

Bertholet, A., "A History of Hebrew Civilization," (transl. by A. K. Dallas), London, 1926

Bevan, E. R. and C. Singer (editors), "The Legacy of Israel," Oxford, 1927

Delaporte, L., "Los Hittites," Paris, 1936

Diringer, D., "The Alphabet," New York, 1948

Finegan, J., "Light from the Ancient Past," Princeton, 1946

Gurney, O. R., "The Hittites," Harmondsworth, 1964

Meek, T. J., "Hebrew Origins," New York, 1936

Moore, G. F., "History of Religions," 2 Vols., New York, 1937

Mendelsohn, I., "Slavery in the Ancient Near East," New York, 1949

Olmstead, A. T., "A History of the Persian Empire," Chicago, 1948

Rogers, R. W., "A History of Ancient Persia," New York, 1929

Sykes, P. M., "A History of Persia," 2 Vols, 3rd ed., London, 1930

<u>North of the Mediterranean</u>

Glotz, G., "The Aegean Civilization," (transl. by M. R. Dobie and E. M. Riley), New York, 1927

Hall, H. R., "The Civilization of Greece in the Bronze Age." London, 1928

Hutchinson, R. W., "Prehistoric Crete," Baltimore, 1963

Huxley, G. L., "Achaeans and Hittites," Oxford, 1960

------, "Crete and the Luwians," Oxford, 1961

Myres, J. L., "Who Were the Greeks?" Berkeley, 1930

Nilsson, M. P., "Homer and Mycenae," London, 1933

[Bibliography continued]

Page, D., "History and the Homeric Illiad," Berkeley, 1959

Person, A. W., "The Religion of Greece in Prehistoric Times," Berkeley, 1942

Starr, C. G., "The Origins of Greek Civilization," New York, 1961

Thomson, G., "Studies in Ancient Greek Society: The Prehistoric Agean," London, 1949

Young, A. M., "Troy and Her Legend," Pittsburgh, 1948

Botsford, G. W. and E. G. Sihler, "Hellenic Civilization," New York, 1920

Gary, M., "The Documentary Sources of Greek History," Oxford, 1927

Ferguson, W. S., "Greek Imperialism," New York, 1913

Grote, G., "A History of Greece," New ed. 12 vols., New York, 1906

Pritchett, W. K., "Studies in Ancient Greek Topography," Berkeley and Los Angeles, 1965, Part I.

Robinson, C. A. Jr., "Alexander the Great," New York, 1949

Tarn, W. W., "Alexander the Great," 2 vols., Cambridge, 1948

Snowden, F. W., "Blacks in Antiquity: A Greco-Roman Experience," Cambridge, 1970

Milne, J. G., "Greek and Roman Coins and the Study of History," London, 1939

Seltman, C. T., "Greek Coins," London, 1933

Seltman, C., "Masterpieces of Greek Coinage," London, 1949

Black, R. S., "Plato's Life and Thought," London, 1949

Field, G. C., "The Philosophy of Plato," London, 1949

Kirk, G. S. and Raven, J. E., "Presocratic Philosophers," Cambridge, 1960

Nilsson, M. P., "A History of Greek Religion," Oxford, 1925

Pearson, L., "Early Ionian Historians," Oxford, 1939

Wells, J., "Studies in Herodotus," Oxford, 1923

Jouquet, P., "Macedonian Imperialism and the Hellenization of the East," (transl. by M. R. Dohie), New York, 1928

McEwan, C. W., "The Oriental Origin of Hellenistic Kingship," Chicago, 1934

Block, R., "The Origins of Rome," New York, 1960

Homo, L., "Primitive Italy and the Beginnings of Roman Imperialism," (transl. by V. G. Childe), New York, 1927

Randall-MacIver, D., "The Etruscians," Oxford, 1927

Baker, G. P., "Hannibal," London, 1930

Boak, A. E. R., "A History of Rome to A. D. 565," 5th ed., New York, 1965

Chapot, V., "The Roman World," New York, 1928

Frank, T., "Roman Imperialism," 2nd ed., New York, 1914

-----, "A History of Rome," New York, 1923

Liddell-Hart, B. H., "A Greater than Napoleon, Scipio Africanus," London, 1927

Mommsen, T., "The History of Rome," 5 vols. new ed., New York, 1903—05

Ormerod, H. A., "Piracy in the Ancient World," Liverpool, 1924

Sculland, H. H., "Scipio Africanus in the Second Punic War," Cambridge, 1930

Thiel, J. H., "Studies in the History of Roman Sea-Power," Amsterdam, 1946

THE LAW OF OPPOSITES: AN INTERPRETATION : by Evelyn Walker.

The deification of man is not a new phenomena. It has existed since the beginning of man in the Nile Valley and other areas of Africa. If, as Frazier has stated, man in his early years worshipped stones and trees, the attributes of such objects were distinctly human [Frazier, THE GOLDEN BOUGH, Vol. I, p. 89]. He has thus personified that which he calls "god [s]" since time immemorial. Is this not the way it should be? Man, in judging all that was around him, could use only himself as a measuring stick. It is only natural that his ideas of divinity reflect what he thought things to be.

It has been stated that the religions of Western Europe as well as Hinduism and Islam of Asia have their foundations in the Egyptian Mystery [Mysteries] System, more specifically, in THE LAW OF OPPOSITES. It is apparent that on examining the theology of Egypt, India and Greece, there are striking similarities in the religious tenets. Some of these similarities will be focused upon in an attempt to further clarify the presumption that just as man came out of the Nile, so did his religion.

The Egyptian religious system has been called by some authors a polytheism, whi makes it unlikely, if not impossible, that the monotheistic religions could have developed c of it. Recent works such as that of professor ben-Jochannan have aided in dissipating this cusation [Dr. Yosef ben-Jochannan],BLACK MAN OF THE NILE AND HIS FAMILY]. Comparative study between the Jesus/Mary/Joseph story and that of Horus/Isis/Osiris have sh that the two bear a striking resemblance, allowing, of course, for factors of geography anc history. Further, comparation of Osiris and Adonis by Frazier in the GOLDEN BOUGH al show similarity in the birth and death of the two. What are the implications of this? At wor the three are coincidental; at best and more likely, the stories are different versions of the same occurance with Osiris being the original story. Thus, if Egypt was polytheistic, so w Rome.

The premise that Egypt was a polytheistic society has further been challenged in I A. Wallis Budge, EGYPTIAN IDEAS OF THE FUTURE LIFE . He maintains that Egypt was a monotheistic society. It is the author's contention that the foundation of the Egyptian theology was monotheistic upon which a polytheistic covering was laid [Budge, p. 10]. In the Precepts of Kaqema and the Precepts of Ptahetep, there is no ambivalence in the number o Gods to whom the writer is refering - he refers to one God. Further, the Maxims of Khenshetep which was composed during the XVIII Dynasty speaks of God in the singular [Budge,

12]. In addition, the Maxims of Khensu-hetep bear a striking resemblance to the TEN COMMANDMENTS of the Hebrew and Christian Bible, also the Moslem Qur'an [Bible]. Such striking evidence would indicate that despite its polytheistic overtones, the religion of Egypt was based solely upon a monotheistic foundation. Further, based on the above, one must at least accept the idea that the Judaeo-Christian religion has some foundation in Egyptian theology. However, form is not enough upon which to base any contention. Two objects may have the same form and be as different as night and day. The real indicator is substance - whether or not the inherent ideas and belief of the two are similar.

Perhaps there is no better way to judge the merits of any religion than by an assessment of the godhead - that is, the Supreme Being upon whom the religion is based. The Egyptian Supreme Being, unlike the Christian godhead, had no name. However, this should not prevent one from assessing his substance; though this point is at present in controversy. The traditional belief has been that Ra was the Supreme Being in the Egyptian religion. However, Maspero, THE DAWN OF CIVILIZATION and Budge, THE EGYPTIAN IDEAS OF THE FUTURE, challenges this assertion. Budge, more so than Maspero, maintains that Ra was the Supreme Representative of the Supreme Being, but not the Supreme Being. The reading of the Maxins of Khensu-hetep and the Percepts would indicate the existence of a Being higher than Ra. For the Judaeo-Christian, he is known as God or Lord.

> "...God is from the beginning, and He hath been from the beginning.
> He hath existed from of old and was when nothing else had being...."

[Budge, p. 20]. The above is a description of the Egyptian Supreme Being, but it could be a description of Lord or Al'lah as well. The Supreme Being for the Egyptians was without description. He was just there. Plato, in relegating intelligence to its highest point, would have called him pure intelligence, pure energy or pure reason. While the Egyptians did not call him as such, it is evident that for them, he was this also. According to Egyptian mythology, the world was created from the spoken word, [Budge, p. 23], of the primeval water. The implication of this is apparent in that the word had to be spoken by a mind. Further, the shape and form of the world was the result of the designs of "the spirit " [Budge, 23]. Again, the concept of the Supreme Being is one of pure intellect or pure energy. It had to be pure because nowhere is the Supreme Being given shape, be it stone or wood. In addition, Budge is certain that the polytheism of Egypt was their way of personifying an immaterial conception - thus, giving shape and form to a part of that conception. This theory holds up when it is realized that the Gods of Egypt were, as the Gods of Greece and Rome, limited in their capacity.

Each deity had certain abilities, none was limitless. It is analogous to a pie that has been sliced into sections - each section represents a part of the pie. Further, the easy acceptance of polytheism is made clearer. Just as the mind has many facets, and the man plays many roles, the foundation of the two is unitary. The same follows for the Supreme Being. The function served by Osiris, Ra, Thoth and others is similar to the function served by Jesus Christ. All are personifications of the formless shape that orders the universe.

Within this same vein, Maspero's description of the creation of Thoth implies that the composition of the god [s] out of pure thought was not an alien concept. Further, the description of the Supreme Being in the Maxims of Khemsu-hetep reveals that "thought" was a very real part of Egyptian theology. Maspero's accusation that Egyptian theologians did not comprehend that thought created the world is an indication of his failure to read beyond the myths. It is also totally illogical that man,whose mind created his religion,would not come to realize that thought was instrumental to his survival.

From the belief in "thought" and "mind," it is only natural that the deification of man followed.... For it is in man's mind that the deification process takes place. In the essay presented, several theories of this process have been advanced. For Pythagoras, the process was: Transmigration, Immortality and Salvation. For Africans, it was: Opposite or conflicting contraries, Transmutation or fluidity of change, and the functional life of the universe caused by the four elements. For Socrates, it was The Doctrine of the Nous and Sonum or The Law of the Greatest Good. It is the writer's contention that all are correct because all are based primarily on the same foundation. They are different versions of the same thing. Is it nc Socrates' Greatest Good, or Pythagoras' Immortality and Salvation, which represents the functional life of the universe?

An examination of the diagram will reveal that the four qualities are part of the four elements. These qualities were symbolic and realistic boundaries of the Egyptian world. As such, they take on special meaning for the people. They are dependent on the earth for existence and they know of an earth that is hot but cooled by the warm, gentle breezes of the Nile. The same follows in life - they know of the day that is long, as is life, and tiring, but they also know of the sweet joys of love and accomplishment. Thus, they could see and feel the contradictions of nature, and within this, the contradictions of man. This may appear to be simplistic, but it is not. The contradictions in nature were apparent, yet nature was not destroyed or thrown into chaos by them. Thus, within nature, there was a uniting of opposite forces which lived in apparent harmony. It seemed only logical that this discovery should be transferred to man since he was part of nature. Moore [Moore, THE BIRTH AND GROWTH OF RELIGION, pp. 8 - 12] maintains that as man develops technologically, his religious beliefs and how he views the world develop as well. For the ancient Egyptians, the four elements and qualities seemed appropiate to explain the world, and as man was a part of that world, it explained him also. However, as man evolved, his theology became more complex as he realized that nature was more complex. Despite its complexity, the union of opposites maintained itself - everything could be broken into cause and effect; the coexistence of opposing forces side by side. This idea is reflected in not only Egyptian mythology, Greek mythology, but also Christianity. For, does not good and evil exist side and by side and are dependent on each for their existence - just as man is dependent on his inner and outer self for existence?

However, one might be led to ask how this principle evolved or involved the deification of man? An examination of the second and third principle of the UNION OF OPPOSITES will help to clarify this point. For man, as for nature, transmutation or change was death. Death was the ultimate change in man; and its occurance altered the physical appearance of man. The function of the universe, according to the Egyptians, was cyclical. That is, the universe was a circle - never ending, never beginning. FIRE, WATER, EARTH, AIR as well as the qualities are shown in the diagram to be interconnected and related. Each flowed into the other. It was necessary that man maintain this fluidity - for was he not part of nature? FIRE, AIR, etc. were physical elements which could and did change their forms. Could not man do the same? But how, and who would guarantee that a change did take place after death? Using his most powerful gift, his mind, man created someone who would see his transformation and a process that would account for this change. It is because "God" is a creation of man's mind that he is personified; that his ultimate form is shapeless as is the mind; and that death MUST occur. It is in this process that "God" becomes divine - he is the ultimate idea of the creation mind. Thus, the Egyptian's idea of "goodness" becomes Plato's idea of "reason." In both cases, reason and goodness are the ideal of man in a given society. Thus, SONOM BONUM or THE GREATEST GOOD must be interpreted as the IDEAL - an IDEAL which is defined by the members of a society.

If we return to the DIAGRAM, this point can be further elaborated upon. In the DIAGRAM, 8 is the symbolic representation of man's elevation to a higher level. Why? It is representative of the cyclical structure of the cosmos. One/half of 8 is 4 which is the symbolic representation of perfection. It is evident that perfection is a necessary prerequisite for the elevation of man to a higher level. In this, two facts become evident: [1] Pythagoras' system of transmutation, transmigration, immortality and salvation are merely a Greek version of this idea, and [2] death is the necessary action which makes this attainment possible.

However, the process of deification or salvation could not just drop out of a hat. First, man had to have something that could exist after death. It could not be the body because it rotted and decayed and it had to be immaterial - a quality. Here again it is the DIAGRAM which serves as a foundation. The FOUR ELEMENTS had FOUR QUALITIES with which they interacted. Thus, there existed physical and mental components in nature and thus in man. This and the power of the human mind was instrumental in developing the soul/mind as the best candidate for the job. Was not the soul/mind like the wind - always present, always changing and never dying? One step in the process had been completed; but what of immortality? It must be remembered that at some point, man did not consider any part of himself immortal - to do so without any rational seemed illogical. Thus, the creation of the RESURRECTION of Osiris and Jesus. It is their RESURRECTION which makes them essential to the religions. The rational for the belief in immortality is accomplished through Osiris being put together by Isis and returning to rule over the kingdom of the dead. Burial diggings have revealed that the ancient Egyptians tore the dead to pieces apparently in the belief that in doing this, they were sure to come back to life [Moore, p. 175]. I would speculate that the early Christians didn't mind being crucified for the same reason. With evolution, this practice was eliminated as man became more sophisticated in his theology.

The human body, as Plato has maintained, is full of weakness, mental and physical. The attainment of divinity - which should be interpreted as becoming part of the universal functioning - is something that man can strive for only on a mental level. As the Egyptians discovered, the human body can never survive nor arise once the body has ceased to function. The inner self can be survived given the proper care and treatment. For Plato, salvation came when the mind controlled the soul and lived as virtuous as possible [Moore, p. 120]. For the Egyptian, it was living the good life. It should be noted that both these ideas were based on keeping in harmony with nature. If one is good and/or virtuous then one is in keeping with nature which counterbalances itself so as to maintain itself in a state of equilibrium. But, this inner self, striving to live a virtuous life, was trapped by its physical body. Death could only release this inner self. Thus, the TRANSMUTATION of life was a prerequisite to the TRANSFORMATION of the soul. This, however, was not enough. Both Egyptians and Western society believe that IMMORTALITY OF THE SOUL was not the end. The SOUL had to be judged - for Egyptians, Osiris judges the "GOODNESS" of the soul; for the Christians, God judged the "VIRTUOUSNESS" of the departed one. If the person measured up to the standards [which were set by man], he had reached perfection and thus became part of the cosmos. For the Egyptians, he traveled across the sky with Ra; for the Christians, he became an angel [which were only extensions of the Supreme Being]. In either case, the SOUL was rewarded by becoming part of the universe, be it pure energy, pure intellect or pure goodness.

There are, of course, variations on the above. However, it is evident the theoretical foundation of the religions of the West are to be found in an analysis of THE LAW OF OPPOSITES. The function of this principal was to keep man in harmony with nature. Out of the search to do this, the deification of man resulted. So it is out of the Nile Valley and Great Lakes High-Cultures came man and his religion.

ANNOTATED BIBLIOGRAPHY

Breasted, James H. ANCIENT TIMES: A HISTORY OF THE EARLY WORLD, New York, Ginn and Company, 1944

Budge, E. A. Wallis. EGYPTIAN IDEAS OF THE FUTURE LIFE, London, K. Paul, Trench, Trubnet, 1899.

Frazier, James. THE GOLDEN BOUGH: A STUDY IN MAGIC AND RELIGION, New York, MacMillan, 1922

Maspero, Gaston. THE DAWN OF CIVILIZATION; EGYPT AND CHALDEA, Translated by M. L. Clure, New York, D. Appleton, 1894.

Moore, George Foot. THE BIRTH AND GROWTH OF RELIGION, New York, C. Scribner's Son, 1923.

Moore, George Foot. HISTORY OF RELIGIONS, New York, C. Scribner's Sons, 1919 - 1919.

Rawlinson, George. HISTORY OF RELIGIONS, New York, C. Scribner's Sons, 1883.

COURSE TEXTBOOK

ben-Jochannan, Yosef. BLACK MAN OF THE NILE AND HIS FAMILY, New York, Alkebu-lan Books Associates, 1972.

OLD TESTAMENT and NEW TESTAMENT [any version]

THE COGNITIVE PATH: by Dorothy Lee Cobb.

Egyptologist-historian -professor Yosef ben-Jochannan has provided a masterful puzzle to us in the form of the ancient African DIAGRAM OF THE LAW OF OPPOSITES. At first glance the DIAGRAM appears to be relatively simple, as it is easy to say that everything in nature has an OPPOSITE, and that these OPPOSITES have certain QUALITIES. However, the form of the DIAGRAM itself; the squares and triangles, the placing of the numbers themselves within the squares and triangles and the QUALITIES of the ELEMENTS have profound meaning that when explicated are succinct methods of explanation of the foundation of the Egyptian system of religion.

During the time of the African High-Cultures situated along the Nile Valley there were two types of religious instruction, EXOTERIC and ESOTERIC. Exoteric teaching was applied to the VULGAR, a term which meant the mass of the people during antiquity. There were only a few who were admitted to the ESOTERIC instruction which allowed initiates into the Mysteries System to learn the symbols of the religion and the philosophy of the religion. It is very interesting to note here that it has been pointed out by historians dealing with so-called "primitive symbolism" that Jesus [the Christ] of the Haribu and his "Twelve Apostles" were representative of this type of closed or ESOTERIC instruction. They were instructed in the Mysteries as can be seen by the feats of magic and healing performed by "the Christ" [anointed]. In fact, the whole life of "the Christ" was set along a "PATH" which was very analogous to the PATH of initiates into the Egyptian Mysteries System. Jesus "the Christ" was called the "SON OF LIGHT",which was the highest grade or level within the Mysteries System, as it represented oneness with the spiritual conciousness. The parables of "the Christ" were a means of shrouding in mystery the meaning which could only be derived by those who were a part of the Mysteries System. All of these facts then definitely lead to Jesus and his Apostles as initiates into the Mysteries and the Bible as being an ESOTERIC document.

From the outset of this paper it is necessary to say that the African DIAGRAM OF THE LAW OF OPPOSITES is so complicated that any student attempting to deal with it is set on a cognitive path of his own. Some of the conclusions I have drawn from the DIAGRAM may indeed be shaky but the path towards understanding of the inner-self has led me along a path from dealing with phallic worship to salvation. I have looked at the DIAGRAM as being indicative of the ESOTERIC SYMBOLS that were used among the Africans of the Nile Valley. If there are seeming contradictions in this paper they may be ascribed to my striving towards a high level of understanding. It took the initiates of the ESOTERICS in antiquity many years to complete their studies and advance to the last high level of development which was the oneness with the spiritual conciousness. The weaknesses exhibited by my reasoning can thereby be forgiven in view of the scant knowledge I possess.

There were three stages through which the life of an African along the Nile Valleys went through as part of the Mysteries System. The first stage was of INITIATION [The Mortals; not yet experienced into the Inner Vision]; ILLUMINATION [The Intelligences; attainment of the Inner Vision]; and PERFECTION [The Creators or Sons of Light; who had become part of spiritual consciousness].

The differing knowledges of those esoterically instructed and the mass of those exoterically instructed led to a tremendous gulf which has widened even more in our generation. It is my personal assumption that the belief in another world on the part of people today stems from their ignorance of the knowledge which was/is held by the priests of religion. Not only is the belief in another world a product of this division of knowledge but all other aspects of religion as we know it today such as repentance, something which was not known by the early practitioners of religion along the Nile Valley. SIN as a concept was unknown. Egyptians believed that both GOOD and EVIL existed within man. This idea of GOOD and EVIL as co-existents was seen in Set-Typhon being the other half of the God Osiris. Therefore there was no SIN and no need for REPENTANCE. Nile Valley man's emphasis instead was upon appeasing the GODS which he did by offering up sacrifices.

I have had an ongoing argument with a budding egyptologist as to my contention that the basis of religion as practised by the Egyptians and all peoples down to the present day is phallic. I have been given books to supposedly disprove my assumption but these books, notably, SYMBOLS, SEX AND THE STARS, have only served to reinforce my ideas. The trouble I had with Busenbark's SYMBOLS, SEX AND THE STARS was his orientation towards Babylonia as the birthplace of man; however, even this fact did not overshadow the information which was supportive of a theory of phallicism being the basis of religion.

The basic question man has asked since the beginning of time has been how he got here. What is the reason for existence is a question on a higher level of abstraction, and one which I believe the early Africans had no difficulty with or reason to ask once they had determined the answer to the "HOW" of existence. In other words, the determination of the "HOW" and further striving for the "WHY" is redundancy to the point of absurdity; one excludes the other. I have difficulty in defining what the Egyptians/Ethiopians and all other Africans along the Nile

Valley held as belief-systems to be called METAPHYSICS despite the fact that their beliefs were intricate and indicated a high degree of intelligence; an intelligence perhaps unequalled since. METAPHISICS, as it strikes me, is a WHITE PHILOSOPHY; because one of the questions asked by metaphysicians is the above-stated "WHY" of existence. The Africans were pragmatists. PRAGMATISM is not synonymous with a state of primacy or a primal state.

In seeking explanations for the "HOW" of his existence man became cognizant of the generative powers of the moon [female] and the sun [male]. Man can be seen as being evolutionary, not in the Darwinian conception of man's descent from primates but rather evolutionary in the various stages of phases which he passes through not only biologically but spiritually; this spirituality ending in the path to the ULTIMATE COGNITION; man deified or man projected outside himself into the universe as God.

The rising and setting of the sun, the different phases of the moon, the seasons which created a death/life condition during the winter upon vegetation and spring and summer which saw a bursting forth of new life, were the means by which man was aided in his attempts to answer the "HOW" of himself.

The answers to the "HOW" appeared to be stated in the LAW OF OPPOSITES which is the name of the matrix presented by professor Yosef ben-Jochannan; a matrix itself being equivalent to the female or mother within which something originates or takes form. Man determined that it was the conjunction of the female and male principles that produced life. Thus Mother Earth and the Sky as Father produced the verdure, animals, and even man himself; or the moon and sun mating produced everything or it was the combination of Fire and Water who were the Grand Father and Grand Mater; all of which broken down simply were representations of the male and female. Having evolved to this stage of COGNITION of the phallic principle, man sought to represent this principle symbolically which led to the creation of the TAU ANKH [Crux Ansata], and the Christian Cross. The TAU T, by containing three parts, the horizontal and the vertical, represented the male principle as the male organ of generation included the phallus and the testicles. The Christian Cross † is simply a variation of the TAU. The Crux Ansata or Ankh of the Egyptians is much more realistic in its depiction of the principle of generation for unlike the TAU or CROSS it has four parts ☥ , the horizontal and the vertical again representing the male but with the addition of the loop or egg which represents the female principle, being shaped like the organ of the woman. It has been pointed out that Roman Catholicism has been the only religion which has recognized the female principle. This they have done through the worship of the "VIRGIN MARY." Nevertheless, the Roman Catholic symbol of religion continues to be the masculine cross.

The creation of symbols also gave rise to the use of numbers containing special meanings. The matrix provided by professor ben-Jochannan contains the numbers one through eight. Simple reasoning will enable us to derive the meaning of the numbers ONE through FOUR by referring back to the TAU and the CRUX ANSATA. Right through the center of the DIAGRAM of the PRINCIPLES OF THE LAW OF OPPOSITES there is a representation of a CROSS which divides a square into four triangles. Inside each triangle there is a number. Triangles are tripartite and all tripartite symbols are representative either of the female principle or taking the lines which form a triangle collectively, are representative of the woman, man and child; the right angle representing man and woman, vertical being man and horizontal woman. The hypothenuse is the child. Although the triangle is tripartite and it was mentioned previously that threes like in the CROSS are representative of the phallus, it is necessary to point out the triangle is also female because when turned upside down it looks like the VAGINA. Greek houses that employ the symbol for Delta don't realize that they are dedicated to phallic worship [Delta Δ , or ∇].

The number "ONE" represents the source of all things; it can be called reason. The number "TWO" signifies male and female, the cause of increase and division. "THREE" is identified with creation or renewal; THREE giving rise to the TRIAD, TRINITY or THREE-GOD HEAD, which was nothing more than the phallus and testicles deified. "FOUR" represents the root of all things, the foundation of nature, and is considered the most perfect number because it represents the conjunction of the male and female principle attesting to the fact that creation can only occur with the union of male and female such union representing them, PERFECTION.

This system of numerology was devised by Africans but like most knowledge was accredited to the WHITES in this instance Pythagoras who had done most of his studying of the mysteries within Egypt. All studies he engaged in outside Egypt were still African as no other race of people at the time had devised a Mysteries System comparable to the Africans.

The numbers FIVE through EIGHT are more difficult to explicate through simple reasoning. The DIAGRAM only goes up to EIGHT because the Egyptians had not devised 9 and 10 during that very early period. According to Busenbark's analysis of the so-called "PYTHAGOREAN SYSTEM," FIVE is the equilibrium. It represents marriage or union of the first masculine and first feminine numbers 3 and 2. SIX is the number of completion. This number is identified with time as the measure of duration. SEVEN, "One of the most venerated and most magical of numbers, the number par excellence among the nations of antiquity. Pythagoras called it the 'vehicle of Life'. It contains body and soul, spirit and matter." [1]

"EIGHT is identified with man's elevation to a higher life or his deliverance from the evils of the present life." [2]

As mentioned earlier, the African DIAGRAM OF THE LAW OF OPPOSITES does not contain the numbers NINE and TEN. They are however included within the Pythagorean System NINE is incompletion because it is one step short of perfection which is 10 or I0, I0 being God From my understanding of the analysis NINE is the last stage of inner striving and 10 represents the culminating point or man's attunement with the cosmos, the highest stage of initiation or the ULTIMATE COGNITION. These last two steps enabled man to formulate the concept of immortality.

Before dealing with man's ideas on IMMORTALITY, it is necessary to say that the elements: AIR, FIRE, WATER, and EARTH and the four qualities: HOT, DRY, WET, and COLD, I took to mean the projection outwards of the phallic principles or man and woman. Th universe mirrored man or earth and the generative principles were the same for the universe as they were for man.

Once man had determined that a creative force, the generative organs, answered the HOW of his existence and he had formed symbols as a means of worshipping the generative principle, the next problem presented to man would be the means of perpetuation of self, or immortality. I understand the number 10 as existing outside of the matrix because it is at this stage that man's mind/soul becomes a part of the cosmos. This theory is valid to me because I equate this with the Great OSIRIS and his ascent up the ladder of Abydos. OSIRIS the man had been murdered by his brother SET-TYPHON. Osiris' body was later dismembered by Set. Isis the wife-sister of Osiris,found all of the members of Osiris except the phallus which had been eaten by the Nile Catfish. It is here that I derive the whole basis of the Egyptian religious system. Because Isis was unable to find the phallus of Osiris she erected a gigantic pillar which was to be worshipped by the people. Of course, this story is a fable which the people invented. Osiris represented the sun and Isis the moon. The reason for the invention of the whole phallic tale was simply man's transference of self outside or what George Ryley Scott called in his book PHALLIC WORSHIP, "Anthropomorphic Cosmogny." Simply put, man gave the sun and moon the qualities and attributes he himself possessed.

The reconstitution of the body of Osiris could not have been complete without the addition of the lost phallus. Just to back up a second however, before the reconstitution of the body of Osiris, Isis had given birth to Horus. If accepting the symbology of Busenbark and Sha Rocco, the fish in the tale who ate the phallus represented the female principle, then the condition for the birth of the son existed as the phallus was conjoined with the female. Also the Great Nile River itself could be taken to represent the female principle or Isis as water is the symbol for the female; bodies of water are often referred to as lifegiving. Horus was the fruit of the principle of generation without whom it would have been impossible for the man Osiris to advance to another level of COGNITION. It was Horus who possessed the magic words and formulas that gave the corpse of the man Osiris life.

On the path to immortality then, man conceptualized a principle of genearation. The union of man and woman was analogous to a death/life state as man and woman as whole entities or units each containing the seeds for reproduction were engaged in the fact of simultaneously dividing and reconstructing themselves. The child produced represented man perfected or man's attainment of a form of immortality. This idea of the child being man's perfection is in complete agreement with the idea of perfection existing on either pole of existence. Man before he is born is a state of perfection and he is in a state of perfection at death, with the in between of man's life. This death being imperfect was not a literal death but was instead figurative.

Horus by a reconstitution of the body of Osiris then became the Great Osiris which represented the culmination of the path of cognition whereby Osiris was united with all his ancestors who had preceded him in death. Taken as part of the cognitive path this uniting with the ancestors was simply being accepted into the priesthood of all those who had successfully gone through the Mysteries System.

The greatest hope held by the Africans along the Nile was that they too could become like Osiris which meant essentially that they were interested in immortality. The Africans saw the state of existence after death as the same as the state of life which would seem to invalidate the conception of immortality that we hold today or the belief in another world; a heaven flowing with milk and honey. The belief held by the Africans of the sameness of existence is indicated by the food, clothing, statutes of slaves and representation of the phallus and small priapic gods buried with prominent citizens as well as ordinary citizens. The inclusion of the priapic statues certainly points to the hope of continued generation on the other side of death. In talking about burials it is interesting to note that according to Sha Rocco the pyramid itself was a sexual symbol of the female organ which would indicate not only the phallic nature of the belief systems held by the Africans, but the belief in a form of rebirth as it could be seen that burial in the pyramid was analogous to the unborn child in the mother's womb. Understanding then the symbolism of pyramids and tombs, it becomes much easier to understand the body of Jesus being placed in a tomb and his ascent after three days. Leaving aside the whole solar argument of the tale of death of Jesus and his resurrection, the reemergence in three days as "the Christ," is similar to customs prevailing in early religions whereby natural structures such as crevices, caverns, etc. by their being considered as the female principle, enable people to pass through the structure bodily thereby being purified as if emerging from the womb of the woman.

As mentioned previously, the CROSS or TAU as the symbol for the Male Organ. Jesus was impaled upon a CROSS upon Mount Calvary; the term "MOUNT" also being phallic in that it was used during antiquity to represent the mons vernis region of the woman. There was therefore represented a conjugal act in this account of Jesus' death. I have a great deal of difficulty in understanding the idea of the conjugal act resulting in death othern than to explain it as I did previously as the loss of identity of the separate male and female principles momentarily and the simultaneous reconstruction of this division; or in considering the path of cognition it would mean that the death or advancement to a higher level of cognition automatically gave birth to the means for an even higher existence or level, which would be contradictory in that there would have been no need for the burial in the tomb. Nevertheless, surfice it to say that the idea of rebirth was symbolized by the pyramids of the Nile Valley High-Cultures and in the account of the Haribu nation by the tomb.

The concepts of the SOUL, the KA and SALVATION are really difficult to understand. The basic problem is the overshadowing of my own religious orientation. I was always taught that the SOUL and BODY were synonymous or ONE. This belief was supoosedly always proven by reference to the Bible's rendering of and "God blew into man's nostrils the breath of life and he became a living soul." The DOCTRINE OF THE NOUS has to do with man's liberation from the body, which has always been figuratively depicted as DEATH, which it is since it leads to a rebirth or awakened state. If this is so, then the mind and soul are synonymous - ONE.

The Egyptian KA was depicted as the double of man. My grandfather, a very learned uneducated man, used to always place a great deal of significance on the SHADOW. It is inexplicable to most people that the human body can cast a shadow. My grandfather always believed that the shadow remained on earth after death. His belief, I feel, is similar to the ideas held by the Africans along the Nile as I understand them: After death man's KA remained on earth.

It was to the Ka that man erected places of worship and wore amulets, so he could appease the Ka of the ancestors. After rereading ben-Jochannan's BLACK MAN OF THE NILE AND HIS FAMILY in an attempt to pull together all these ideas into some kind of workable whole, perhaps then too the Ka was also representative of the Nous or the mind liberated. As the intellect is one of the governing principles of existence, it would be reasonable to assume that it exists after death also.

Salvation as I understand it within the context of the African belief in immorality through the liberation of the mind is very different from the salvation taught by Judaism and Christianity. According to Judaeo-Christianity man exists in state of sin because of the original SIN or the Matherian jingle of "In Adam's Fall Sinned We All"; the ORIGINAL SIN being no less than the sex act. Just as an addendum here, an explanation of the two conflicting accounts of creation in the BOOK OF GENESIS as mentioned by ben-Jochannan in his work "Understand ing the African Philosophical Concept Behind the Diagram of the Law of Opposites" is that the accounts represent two conflicting religious philosophies. The first account was very phallic in nature which was a Judaic carry-over from the African religious system.

The Mosaic Laws as passed down by the Haribu leader Moses, introduced into Judaeo-Christianity a trend against phallic worship. It is necessary to say however that even with the Mosaic Laws man had not advanced to the state of an abstract God concept such as the one in existence now. It is interesting to note the difficult time that the religious Haribu leaders had in their attempts to stamp out phallic worship. What happened was that phallic worship and the religion of YAHWEH co-existed through the accounts in the OLD TESTAMENT. Moses himself supposedly received the laws upon Mount Sinai. As mentioned previously, the mount was used as an esoterical symbol for the female organ or the fringe. Evidently, this meant that the foundation upon which the laws were promulgated was phallic regardless of how relentless the attempts were made to stamp out the practice.

The second account of the creation in GENESIS I take to represent the Mosaic Crusade against sex. Obviously, the time span between the two reditions was great.

To go back to the idea of salvation, salvation in the Judaeo-Christian context means to be saved or redeemed because of the imperfection of man caused by the Original Sin, the Original being determined by the purists as disobedience to God. GOOD and EVIL became distinct qualities as personified by God and the Devil. The African of the Great Lakes region did not have this problem of having to be saved because of an original sin which caused imperfection among the whole human species. The African system of religion was in existence thousand of years before the fictional account of the Fall of Man. The idea of sex and generation were the foundation of the African religious system. The triad itself had the destroyer aspect included within it; man was neither good nor evil but both. The African had nothing from which to be saved. Even the account of the 42 NEGATIVE CONFESSIONS performed by the dead before Osiris and the other gods in the Judgment Scene had nothing to do with confessions of sin, but were rather statements as to the dead's relations with others while yet alive or passing throug the cognitive path. The dead had attempted in life to attain as nearly as possible a state of perfection as to be judged and accepted into the Body of Gods before the Great Osiris.

Derived meanings from the Haribu Bible seem to make up the bulk of Judaeo-Christia philosophy as we know it today. An indication of this is not only the striving for salvation to negate the ORIGINAL SIN but also the ideas of resurrection and punishment for the wicked. It has been pointed out that nowhere in the PENTATEUCH is it indicated that YAHWEH ever warned Adam, Noah, Abraham or Moses of the end of the present world or a day of resurrection or punishment for the wicked.

In an attempt to come to some conclusion on the explication of the African DIAGRAM OF THE LAW OF OPPOSITES, it seems that two or three levels of understanding can be ascertained. The primary level is that the DIAGRAM explains that everything in nature is contradictory, or that it contains its own negation, or simply that everything has an opposite. Secondly, the DIAGRAM can be looked upon as being an esoteric symbol to explain the religious system of the ancient Africans and lastly, that the symbols and numbers employed point to the phallic nature of the Egyptian/Ethiopian religious system.

FOOTNOTES:

1. Ernest Busenbark, SYMBOLS, SEX AND THE STARS, p. 243

2. IBID., p. 243

BIBLIOGRAPHY:

ben-Jochannan, Yosef, BLACK MAN OF THE NILE AND HIS FAMILY, Alkebu-lan Books Associates, New York, 1972

Budge, Wallis A., OSIRIS AND THE EGYPTIAN RESURRECTION, Vols. I and II, G. P. Putman Sons, New York,

Busenbark, Ernest, SYMBOLS, SEX AND THE STARS, The Truth Seeker Co., Inc., New York, 1949

[bibliography continued]

Campbell, Joseph. PAGAN AND CHRISTIAN MYSTERIES, Harper and Row, New York, 1955

de-Graft Johnson, J. C. AFRICAN GLORY, London, 1954

Diop, Cheikh Anta [ed. and transl. by Mercer Cook], THE AFRICAN ORIGIN OF CIVILIZATION: MYTH OR REALITY, Lawrence Hill and Co., New York, 1974

Frazer, Sir James. THE GOLDEN BOUGH, London, 1930 [13 vols.]

Howard, Clifford. SEX WORSHIP: AN EXPOSITION OF THE PHALLIC ORIGIN OF RELIGION, Chicago Medical Book Company, Chicago, 1902

Maspero, Gaston. LIFE IN ANCIENT EGYPT AND ASSYRIA, D. Appleton and Co., New York, 1892

Moiti, John S. CONCEPTS OF GOD IN AFRICA, Praeger Publishers, New York, 1970

Rocco, Sha. THE MASCULINE CROSS AND ANCIENT SEX WORSHIP, Commonwealth Co., New York, 1904

Scott, George R. PHALLIC WORSHIP, London: Luxor Press Ltd., 1966

Smith, Homer W. MAN AND HIS GODS, Little Brown and Company, Boston, 1955

Snowden, Frank W. BLACKS IN ANTIQUITY: A GRECO-ROMAN EXPERIENCE, Cambridge, 1970

Steiner, Rudolf. CHRISTIANITY AS MYSTICAL FACT AND THE MYSTERIES OF ANTIQUITY, Rudolf Steiner Publications, Inc., 1961

Westropp, Hodder M. PRIMITIVE SYMBOLISM AS ILLUSTRATED IN PHALLIC WORSHIP OR THE REPRODUCTIVE PRINCIPLE, George Redway Publishers, London

Westropp, Hodder M. and Wake C. Staniland, ANCIENT SYMBOL WORSHIP, J. W. Bouton, New York, 1874

Yarker, John. NOTES ON THE SCIENTIFIC AND RELIGIOUS MYSTERIES OF ANTIQUITY,

COURSE TEXTBOOK:

ben-Jochannan, Yosef. BLACK MAN OF THE NILE AND HIS FAMILY, Alkebu-lan Books Associates, New York, 1972

OLD TESTAMENT and NEW TESTAMENT [any version]

REFLECTIONS ON THE WINTER SOLSTICE: by Calvin Birdsong.

I'm free,
I'm free,
And freedom tastes of reality
...You've been told so many times before,
Messiah's point you to the door,
but no one had the guts to leave the temple

"Tommy" [The Who]

I think I could turn and live with animals,
they are so placid and self-contained.
I stand and look at them long and long.
They do not sweat and whine about their condition.
They do not lie awake and weep for their sins.
They do not make me sick discussing their duty to God.
Not one is dissastisfied, not one is demented with the
mania of owning things,
Not one kneels to another, nor to his kind that lived
thousands of years ago,
Not one is respectable or unhappy over the whole earth.

Walt Whitman

Hey everybody, let me tell you bad news,
Hey everybody, let me tell you bad news,
Hey everybody, let me tell you bad news/
You're not too smart,
you ain't nothing,
Nothing but rythm and blues.

James Brown

Father, open our eyes,
that we may see, to follow thee.
Oh Lord grant us thy lovin' peace,
And let all dissension cease.
Let our faith, each day increase,
And master-Lord, please,
OPEN OUR EYES, OPEN OUR EYES.

Leon Lumkins

Yes, I have cherished my "demagogue" role. I know
that societies have often killed the people
who have helped to change those societies.
And if I die having brought any light,
having exposed any meaningful truth that will
help to destroy the racist cancer that is
malignant in the body of America - then all
credit is due to Al'lah. Only the mistakes have been mine

Malcolm "X"

Many scientists believe that no truly matter or energy has come into being since the beginning of the universe. The implication of this belief is two-fold. First, as part of an enclosed whole, all phenomenon are interelated. Secondly, that being part of an interelated whole no phenomenon can transcend the dynamics of that whole - History.

It is with this perspective that we approach an analysis of UNDERSTANDING THE AFRICAN PHILOSOPHICAL CONCEPT BEHIND THE "DIAGRAM OF THE LAW OF OPPOSITES," a paper which the students in Course: AS and RC 510 - Historiography And Source was given by Professor Yosef ben-Jochannan to read, criticize and extend as we cover the entire work in the "Outline Essay" [pages 1 - 21, with specific instructions on page 17, etc.].

The PAPER seeks the nature of validity in the interelationship of POWER and TRUTH; specifically the process by which the complex theosophical and philosophical concepts developed by the people of Alkebu-lan and manifested by them in the DIAGRAM OF THE LAW OF OPPOSITES stolen by the southern Europeans who used them to build their own High-Culture. This High-Culture subsequently passed the teachings of the Africans to the Northern Europeans who built their own industrial High-Culture, based upon the physical as well as the philosophical exploitation of Africa and her peoples.

Yet in seeking validity in the nature of power and truth,we must remember that both are part of the inter-related whole of nature. If power is ultimately a function of energy, we have noted that energy in nature is a continuous whole, which manifests itself in different forms [mechanical, electrical, chemical, etc.] at different levels. Also, if nothing can transcend the development of the whole, then TRUTH, that which is functional reality, cannot transcend the overall pattern of history.

If then POWER and TRUTH are both part of a related whole it would seem that TRUTH cannot transcend POWER, but neither can POWER transcend TRUTH. So if we analyze the thesis that ancient Afrikans [Africans] developed the TRUTHS upon which High-Culture is built, we must note that no contemporary POWER can completely transcend or negate on going realities of history. In fact, if it is a great POWER such as the industrial High-Culture we live in today in the U.S., it will have had to subsume a great deal of those TRUTHS the Afrikans developed and reflect them constantly.

These findings lend both a methodological approach and an analytical insight to us. Methodologically it supports the view that the best test of a theory is not in specific experimentation but in its efficiency as a building block of further knowledge. In short the former "X" factor becomes a known quantity substantial enough to be used as a basis for comparison with further unknown phenomenon; the development of another theory. Analytically we see tha any theory can best test it's hypothesis against the thesis of the contemporary enviroment, which reflects the truth of history.

This author is currently engaged in an ongoing process of developing theory of history which seeks to find what Theodore Rozak calls, "the locus of reality" in social developmen Currently there is a split in the BLACK LIBERATION MOVEMENT between those that feel the locus of social reality is found in the outside, material environment [Marxist] and those who feel it lies more in the internal, innate, cultural reality of individuals [Nationalists].

My hypothesis is that the locus of social reality rests, as all reality does, in nature; that is, the whole of natural universe, and the nature, or character of that whole's development. Also, that this natural reality moves thru the psychodynamics of individuals and groups to the material enviroment which they create and sustain. In this view the same pattern of energy flows through the development of an individual thats through group development.

This perspective then has two components, individual psychology as Micro-History, and history as Macro-Psychology. As a test of this concepts ongoing validity, we find them explored by two Euro-American social scientists dis-interested in any BLACK LIBERATION theory of history, Arthur Janov and Erik Erikson.

Dr. Janov has developed a Primal Theory of individual development out of radical psycho-therapy observations and tests. Briefly, Janov see's perhaps the most motivating factor in human behaviour as the Primal dysfunction between the intense biological and psychological needs of an infant and its often insensitive enviroment. Since many needs are not met directly, they must be fulfilled by the individual symbolically. It is this symbolization, creative or destructive, which is the motive force in human culture. Primal theory, a quantifiable, rational process is a historical view of individual development which shows how nature, manifested in the organism as needs, shapes behaviour even when the needs are repressed from consciousness.

In "Young Man Luther" Erik Erikson showed how the historical development of the Protestant religion and the historical phenomenon of the Reformation grew out of the intrapsychic development of one man, Martin Luther. One could also imply from Erikson's work that the Psychology of an individual is shaped by psycho-cultural patterns of a particular grou such as Germanic Europeans. This psychological view of historical development we call Marco-Psychology.

Nothing can transcend history, ancient or contemporary. This paper was written near the WINTER SOLSTICE of 1974, traditionally a time of celebrations, and of endings. If the ancient Afrikans developed on-going TRUTHS of history we should find them reflected even in this end-of-the-term, holiday season.

The first psycho-historical study this author considered in relation to the work of Dr. ben-Jochannan was to examine the psycho-historical basis for the proclivity of Afrikans in America for the Christian religion. This author found that even I myself, an aspiring BLACK THEORIST, find the archtypical Christian oratorio, "MESSIAH," by George Frederic Handel comforting and at times inspiring. However, if Afrikan people created the basic concepts upon which Christianity is built, then a psycho-historical thesis of unconscious recognition by Afrikan people of basic Afrikan themes in Christianity is a simple exploration. We have said that the proof of this hypothesis would be a recognized continuity between the concepts of the DIAGRAM OF THE LAW OF OPPOSITES and the content of Christian teachings.

"MESSIAH," written by Handel in 1740 in the space of 23 days is, in itself, one of the highest expressions of European culture. It is a highly dynamic combination of secular musical form with sacred verse that seeks the deeper meanings of both. It is this unique form which highlights the ancient Afrikan concepts that seem to shine thru this 18th century oratorio, at least to this writer, the reader can judge for him or herself:

"Conflicting Contraries" -

"Why do nations furiously rage together?
And why do the people imagine such a vain Thing?
The Kings of the earth rise up and the rulers
take counsel together against the Lord, and His
Anointed."

"Transmutation" -

"Behold, I tell you a mystery; We shall not all sleep;
but we shall all be changed, in a moment,
in the twinkling of an eye,
At the last trumpet."

"The Functional life of the universe caused by the four Elements" -

"Thus saith the Lord of Hosts:
Yet once a little while and I will shake the heavens,
and the earth, the sea, and the dry land;
and I will shake all nations,
And the desire of all nations shall come."

"But who may abide the day of his coming?
And who shall stand when he appeareth?
For He is like a refiners fire."

"Supreme Good" -

"Hallelujah; for the Lord God omnipotent reigneth.
The kingdom of this world is become the kingdom of our Lord,
And of his Christ; and He shall reign for ever and ever.
King of Kings and Lord of Lords, HALLELUJAH!

"Process of Purification" -

"The trumpet shall sound, and the dead shall be raised,
incorruptible, and we shall be changed."

"Transmigration of the Soul" -

"For now is Christ risen from the dead,
the first-fruit of them that sleep."

"Deification" -

"Foe unto us a Child is born, unto us, a Son is given,
And the government shall be upon His soulder;
And His name shall be called, Wonderful, Counselor,
The Mighty God, the Everlasting Father,
The Prince of peace."

"Union of Opposites" -

"Behold, a virgin shall conceive, and bear a son,
and shall call his name Emmanuel;
GOD WITH US."

"Immortality of the Soul" -

"I know my redemer liveth and that He shall
stand at the latter day upon the earth:
And though worms destroy this body yet in
my flesh shall I see God."

"Salvation" [!] -

"Worthy is the Lamb that was slain, and hath
redeemed us to God by His blood, to receive
power and riches and wisdom and strength, and
honour and glory and blessing."

Together the above concepts form what Dr. ben-Jochannan calls "The Deification of Man." In another PAPER I ventured that in this process human beings personify the forces of the universe, the rationality of natural historical development, into Gods and project outward as a symbolic means of communication with their own suppressed feelings and needs.

If this process is an ongoing function of human adaptation then it is logical that Afrikans, the prototype humans who developed the prototype of High-Culture, would be the first to discover these concepts. Psycho-historically we see that the Afrikan concepts of theology, as reflected in "MESSIAH", go beyond any doctrine, dogma, or even Psycho-culture, to speak to basic human needs:

-"Confort ye, Comfort ye my people, saith your God;
speak ye comfortably to Jerusalem;
And cry unto her, that her warfare is accomplished,
that Her iniquity is pardoned."

-"He shall feed His flock like a shephard;
And He shall gather the lambs with his arms,
and carry them in His bosom,
And gently lead those that are with young."

-"Then shall the eyes of the blind be opened
And the ears of the deaf unstoppeth.
Then shall the lame man leap as a hart,
And the tongue of the dumb shall sing."

It is these needs, for comfort, peace, forgiveness, health, gentleness, leadership, and to be held at the bosom, that often had to be suppressed from consciousness by human beings in order to survive in an imperfect enviroment. Janov tells us that such suppressed feelings and needs circulate thru the nervous system below the level of consciousness, causing a tension which drives individuals to unconsciously attempt to satisfy their suppressed needs symbolically.

In the "Deification of Man" we see a philosophical model of this split. Consciousness is projected into a God that controls nature, feelings. We see then that this process is essentially means of rationalizing the necessity for the human race to control its needs and channel the resulting tension into the creation of a High-Culture that would "PREPARE...THE WAY OF THE LORD, MAKE STRAIGHT IN THE DESSERT A HIGHWAY...FOR...GOD.

December is also a time of endings. While marking final PAPERS for a class which studied Black social movements I was struck by two dealing with the conversion experiences of Malcolm "X." During a recent discussion about deification an associate asked; why had'nt Malcolm "X" been deified by Black people? The two PAPERS on Malcolm's conversion; first too Sacred, then too Secularly Black Nationalist, but a type of dynamic, analytical deification.

They were deifications in that they recognize that Malcolm's experience is at once the chief motivating force and the prototypic model for the rise of Black Nationalism in the 1960's. The Black students were analytical in that they sought the emperical, psychological, reasons for Malcolm's conversions. This analytical deification is dynamic in that it draws power from an archtypic, Marco-Psychological concept, deification, and channels that energy into an analysis that furthers human understanding and development.

The PAPERS also opened to me the deep analytical implications of Malcolm's Micro-History. Traditional psychological theory can hardly begin to analyze the pain caused by the traumas of Malcolm's early life; the night riders harrassing his pregnant Mother [tension is transferred from a woman to the fetus she carries],his Father's murder, his relationship with his Mother, the breaking up of his family, his Mother's institutionalization, and his early experiences with insensitive Euro-Americans.

Recently, while re-recording some tapes of Malcolm's speeches, I had my first opportunity to hear, rather than read, Malcolm's message at length. I was struck by the power and emotion of the man's voice. Erikson wrote in "YOUNG MAN LUTHER" that within every great person of history was/is a powerful conflict which combines dialectically to produce a significant social, as well as personal synthesis; Malcolm was the epitome of this theory.

Having at times a narrow vision, Janov has written that"Neaurosis is born in the Mind of the Parent" in The Feeling Child. He fails to see that the parent is shaped by the society in which they live, which is in turn developed according to the needs of nature to transform itself. In Malcolm's life we see a clash of natural, historical forces and tendencies resulted in both a Marco-Psychological and Micro-Historical synthesis. This helps us to understand how the deified life provides a model for the type of individual transformations which produce and sustain social evolution in it's role within the whole of natural development.

Still, much of this is conjecture; it is perhaps fitting that I should end this analysis with a commitment to further analysis of Malcolm's probable Micro-history in order to confirm and specify the above hypothesis.

One characteristic of a natural phenomenon is it self-regenerative abiltiy. The phrase, "THE STRUGGLE CONTINUES" is an indication that the Black liberation struggle is basically a function of nature, which though often difficult and slow, is ultimately good, and just, and continuous. In celebrating the WINTER SOLSTICE human beings recognize the ultimate victory of life over death in nature, by deifying themselves they show how the forces within them are a model of the forces of history. So as Black scholars we must struggle to understand ourselves, so that we may understand history, in order to bring that ultimate goodness and justice of NATURE, POWER and TRUTH, to bear in this world. The study continues.

BIBLIOGRAPHY:

Birdsong, Calvin.ANOTHER STORY [unpublished Research Paper], Cornell University, Ithaca, New York, 1974

-------- FOR OUR CHILDREN'S CHILDREN [unpublished Research Paper], Cornell University, Ithaca, New York, 1974

Canty, Susan.THE CONVERSION OF MALCOLM "X" [unpublished Research Paper], Cornell University, Ithaca, New York, 1974

Erikson, Erik.YOUNG MAN LUTHER, W. W. Norton and Co., New York, 1970

Janov, Authur.THE PRIMAL SCREAM, Medallion Books, New York, 1969

--------- THE ANATOMY OF MENTAL ILLNESS, Medallion Books, New York, 1971

---------THE PRIMAL REVOLUTION, Simon and Schuster, New York, 1972

--------- THE FEELING CHILD, Simon and Schuster, New York, 1973

Granger, Jorman.THE CONVERSION OF MALCOLM "X" [unpublished Research Paper], Cornell University, Ithaca, New York, 1974

ben-Jochannan, Yosef.BLACK MAN OF THE NILE AND HIS FAMILY, Alkebu-lan Books Associates, New York, 1972

Handel, George Frederic.MESSIAH, London, 1740

Roszak, Theodore, THE MAKING OF A COUNTER-CULTURE, Doubleday Books, Garden, City, L. I., New York, 1964

Haley, Alex. AUTOBIOGRAPHY OF MALCOLM X, Grove Press, New York, 1965

COURSE TEXTBOOK:

ben-Jochannan's BLACK MAN OF THE NILE AND HIS FAMILY,Alkebu-lan Books Associates, New York, 1972

OLD TESTAMENT, NEW TESTAMENT [any version].

POSTSCRIPT TO THE "FINAL PAPERS" OF WALKER, COBB AND BIRDSONG: by ben-Jocha

Now,I too will be philosophical. But first, unless we are very careful indeed the entire premise within the "FINAL PAPERS" of these STUDENTS could be totally misread at least, and desperately misunderstood and/or misinterpreted at worst. For example: Birdsong's analysis of Handel's "MESSIAH" on pages 40 and 41 requires an open-minded visualization of all the AFRICANISMS that transcends the theosophical and philosophical teachings inherent in the Mysteries System's hymns, prays, proverbs, confessions, laws, etc. that were edited, converted and adopted by the Haribus [Hebrews, Israelites, Jews, etc.] of Asia and Alkebu-lan d ing their sojourn in Ta-Merry, Ta-Nehisi, Meröe, Itiopi, Lebus and other Nile Valley [Blue White] High-Cultures formed the foundation for their PENTATEUCH [Comesh, Holy Torah, O Testament, etc.]; then by the Greeks of Europe who compounded them into what most "Weste ers" call "GREEK PHILOSOPHY" today; and of course, through the "Most Holy and Sacred Sc tures" of the African/Asian/European Christian BIBLE [New Testament] that was originally c ated and developed in Ta-Merry [Kimit, Qamt, Sais, Mizrain, Egypt, etc.] and Ta-Nehisi [Z Sudan, etc.]; all from their origin along the Great Lakes of Central Alkebu-lan ["Africa"].

He has broken down each concept into the "PRINCIPLES" expressed in the "DIAGRAM C THE LAW OF OPPOSITES," giving each a subtitle that depicts its highest theosophical and m physical meaning. Needless to say much more infinite detailing and comprehension could have been brought forward; but his "FINAL PAPER" would have had to at least become a separate volume all of its own.

Walker's subjectivity with respect to "MAN" being in fact "GOD," at least GODLIKE, te poignantly, what she is highlighting is that the "GOD-KINGS" of Ta-Merry and other Nile Vall High-Cultures religions, like their equals in the Yoruba and Voodoo religions of West Alkebu- along with those of the Druid and Witchcraft religions of Europe, were no more and no less "T DIVINERS" than the "GOD-KINGS" we address as Jehovah [Ywh], Jesus "the Christ" or Al'lah day. She made all of this very clear in the beginning of her "FINAL PAPER" [page 22 this vol when she wrote the following:

"THE DEIFICATION OF MAN IS NOT A NEW PHENOMENA".

Just as we, "MAN" [male and female], have made "SAINTS" of "MAN," equally as "SAINTS" been made into "GODS," the process down through the centuries will continue into the future c differing in theosophics and semantics. Thus for said "GODS"; have we not given them "FORM ELEMENTS, QUALITIES," etc. like "MAN"? Certainly; we even declared that:

"GOD IS A JEALOUS GOD, GOD SMYTHE THE EGYPTIANS, JESUS WHIPPED THE MONEY CHANGERS OUT OF THE TEMPLE, GOD RESTED ON THE SEVENTH DAY, GOD IS A SPIRIT AND MUST BE WORSHIP AS A SPIRIT, JESUS WEPT,"

.tc., etc., etc., ad infinitum.

Cobb, on the other hand, brings the entire purpose for the "DEIFICATION OF MAN" to the ›oint where we are most likely to be condemned as she articulates the GODLINESS OF SEXUAL NTERCOURSE, CONCEPTION or PREGNANCY, CHILD-BARING and CHILD-BIRTH; all of ›hich I would call PROCREATION, but which she prefers to designate as PHALLIC REGENERA-ΊΟΝ in context with academic language.

Certainly it will be Cobb's analysis of the meaning of our text which may bring about the nost adverse reactions; this due to our Judaeo-Christian/Greek-centric puritanical ethics about EXUAL INTERCOURSE, most of which stems from "ADAM AND EVE IN THE GARDEN OF DEN" with the "FORBIDDEN FRUIT" and/or "VIRGIN MARY'S IMMACULATE CONCEPTION" llegories in the OLD TESTAMENT and NEW TESTAMENT respectively. Of course, I will only se two of the most common terms in which to document this conclusion of mine; thus:

"BASTARD" and/or "ILLEGITIMATE"

hild and/or children. Both of these reflect our ANTI-DIVINITY OF MAN and ANTI-SEXUAL IN-'ERCOURSE attitude. Yet, the fact remains that on each birthday we have our FESTIVAL TO EXUAL INTERCOURSE or "PHALLIC WORSHIP." Of course, not consciously; but is it not the IAN'S PHALLIC ORGAN that is the means by which another "MAN" is ORIGINATED - "CRE-.TED"? And, is it not the PHALLIC ORGAN of the WO-"MAN" that is the coupling "OPPOSITE" hich nurtures "MAN'S" DIVINE CREATION - their CHILD, who is...

CREATED/MADE IN THE IMAGE OF THE DIVINE INTELECT, LAW/GOD

ithin the same context as the following extract from the "Sacred and Most Holy Scriptures" we nd in the FIRST BOOK OF MOSES [Genesis], Chapter 1, Verse 26:

"LET US MAKE MAN IN OUR IMAGE, AFTER OUR LIKENESS,"

:c., etc., etc. ?

If at all the first "DIVINE CREATION OF MAN" was by a "DIVINE INTELIGENCE" other an "MAN" himself; certainly since that original it has been "MAN," you and I, who had to con-nue this "DIVINE CREATIVITY" from then to the present. Thus, should there be any doubt that)IVINE CREATION" and "PHYSICAL EVOLUTION", like MIND and INTELIGENCE, are in fact)NE" or "GOD"? This is what Cobb has so briliantly articulated in her own words.

It is this, in the total essence of each and every word stated in these STUDENTS hypotheses, at UNDERSTANDING THE AFRICAN BACKGROUND BEHIND THE "DIAGRAM OF THE LAW OF

OPPOSITES" calls upon all of us to examine, equally the "FOUR QUALITIES" and "FOUR ELEMENTS" expressed by and within the "DIAGRAM OF THE PRINCIPLE [or Law] OF OPPOSITES". Truly it is "IMMORTALITY" we hope for when we speak of "RESURRECTION" and/or "THE HEREAFTER". And with "RESURRECTION" or "REINCARNATION" the entire concept is purely one of...

"THE DEIFICATION OF MAN"...;

YOU! AND I!; MAYBE?

Prefatory Note: In GENESIS ii, Verses 8 - 15 we find the following about the LORD GOD and HIS "great works" during the period when HE was "... CREATING EVERYTHING, AND THE LAWS THEREOF...," etc., that the CONTINENT OF ETHIOPIA [Africa, etc., page xxvi in ben-Jochannan's BLACK MAN OF THE NILE AND HIS FAMILY] was declared by the same "LORD GOD" to be part and parcel of "THE GARDEN OF EDEN"; thusly:

8. And the Lord God planted a garden eastward in Eden; and there he put the man whom he had formed.
9. And out of the ground made the Lord God to grow every tree that is pleasant to the sight, and good for food; the tree of life also in the midst of the garden, and the tree of knowledge of good and evil.
10. And a river went out of Eden to water the garden; and from thence it was parted, and became into four heads.
11. The name of the first is Pi-son: that is which compasseth the whole land of Hav-i-lah where there is gold.
12. And the gold of that land is good: there is bedlium and the onyx stone.
13. And the name of the second river is Gi-hon: the same is it that compasseth the whole land of E-thi-o-pi-a.
14. And the name of the third river is Hid-de-k that is it which goeth toward the east of As-syr- And the fourth river is Eu-phra-tes.
15. And the Lord God took the man, and put him into the garden of E-den to dress it and keep it.

But we are reminded to be very careful of the allegories, myths, poetics, historics, etc. about the LORD GOD in the "HOLY SCRIPTURES" as seen through careful scrutiny in the following from John G. Jackson's GOD, MAN AND CIVILIZATION, pages 155 - 156, and Winwood Reade's THE MARTYRDOM OF MAN, also ben-Jochannan's THE BLACK MAN'S RELIGION..., etc. Volume II - III, page vii:

> This brings us to the character of the Creator. We must beg to observe again that we describe not the actual Creator, but the popular idea of the Creator. It is said that the Creator is omnipotent and also that he is benevolent. But one proposition contradicts the other. Again, either sin entered the world against the will of the Creator, in which case he is not omnipotent, or, it entered with his permission, in which case it is his agent, in which case, he selects sin, in which case he has a preference for sin, in which case he is fond of sin, in which case he is sinful. It is certain that the feelings of the created have in no way been considered. If, indeed, there were a judgment day, it would be for man to appear at the bar not as a criminal, but as accuser. What has he done that he should be subjected to a life of torture and temptation? God might have made us all happy and he has made us all miserable. Is that benevolence? God might have made us all pure and he has made us all sinful. Is that the perfection of morality? If I believed in the existence of this man-created God, of this divine Nebuchadnezzar, I would say, "You can make me live in your world, O Creator, but you cannot make me admire it, you can load me with chains, but you cannot make me flatter you; you can send me to hell-fire, but you cannot obtain my esteem. And if you condemn me, you condemn yourself. If I have committed sins, you invented them, which is worse. If the watch you have made does not go well, whose fault is that? Is it rational to damn the wheels and springs?"[1]

Let me elaborate on the main issue in this volume: THE DOCTRINE OF THE LAW OF OPPOSITES and THE DIAGRAM OF THE LAW OF OPPOSITES. Thus is the "FINITE" and its relationship to the "INFINITE, ODD" with respect to "EVEN", and "NEGATIVE" against "POSITIVE"; these are the basic factors involved in this entire "DOCTRINE" the indigenous Africans of the great Nile River Valley High-Cultures created and developed following their migration from their abode around the Great Lakes areas of Central Alkebu-lan. They are the basics from the TEACHINGS that were equally developed in the MYSTERIES SYSTEM of the GRAND LODGE OF LUXOR and its SUBORDINATE LODGES listed below:

SUBORDINATE LODGES OF THE GRAND LODGE OF LUXOR

1. Palestine [at Mt. Carmel]	10. Rhodes
2. Assyria [at Mt. Herman in Lebanon]	11. Delphi
3. Babylon	12. Miletus
4. Media [near the Red Sea]	13. Cyprus
5. India [at the banks of the Ganges River]	14. Corinth
6. Burma	15. Crete
7. Athens	16. Cush [Itiopi, Ethiopia]
8. Rome [at Elea]	17. Monomotapa [South Africa]
9. Croton	18. Zimbabwe [Rhodesia]

LUXOR was destroyed by fire, burnt to the ground, in the year c. 548 B.C.E. It was set aflame by foreigners, who were jealous of the indigenous Africans ["Negroes,"et al] knowledge of the "MYSTERIES" taught in the Osirica - which included all of the above mentioned disciplines. [See John Kendrick's, ANCIENT EGYPT, Book II, p. 363; Eva B. Sandford's, THE MEDITERRANEAN WORLD, pp. 135 - 139; Yosef ben-Jochannan's, AFRICA: MOTHER OF "WESTERN CIVILIZATION", Chapter IX].

It is from this source that Pythagoras learnt what he passed on to his contemporary European Greeks in Greece [Pyrrhus, Athenia, etc.], and they in turn to their students all the way down to the current Europeans and European-Americans. Thus we also find Heraclitus' response from the Africans of Ta-Merry TEACHINGS about "FIRE" [pyr, sol, God Ra, etc.]" as "THE SOURCE OF CREATION". He also saw "STRIFE" as "THE SEPARATION OF PHENOMENA", and "HARMONY" as "THE RESTORATOR OF BOTH TO EQUILIBRIUM" in "THE ORIGINAL POSITION" [see William Turner's HISTORY OF PHILOSOPHY, page 53, and Yosef ben-Jochannan's AFRICA: MOTHER OF "WESTERN CIVILIZATION", pages 411 - 451].

Plato tried to clarify what he believed to be an explanation for "NATURE"; like Socrates attempt at proving the Egyptians TEACHING about "THE IMMORTALITY OF THE SOUL", using "THE THEORY OF IDEAS" and "THE DIAGRAM OF THE LAW OF OPPOSITES" to demonstrate his proof. Herein the STUDENTS discovered one of the major reasons for denying that the so-called "NEGROES, BANTUS", etc. were/are as much "THE EGYPTIANS" as those we are/were taught are/were "SEMITES, CAUCASOIDS, NILOTS, NEGROIDS", etc.; the same being equally true with respect to the "ETHIOPIANS" as other INDIGENOUS AFRICANS North and South of the Sahara, the vast majority having been very similar to these shown below on this page:

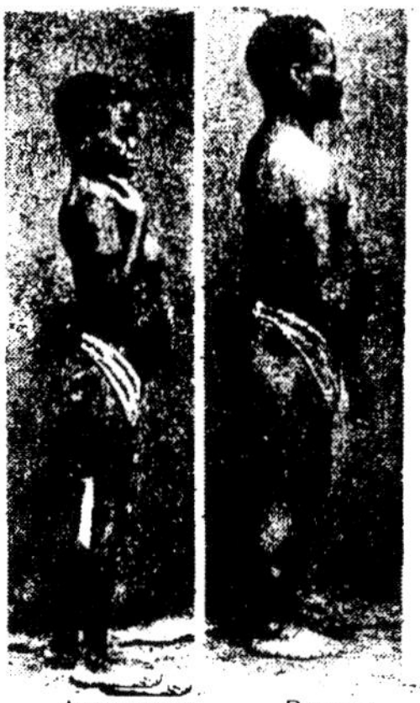

AMOORIAPE BOHANI

"Reproduced by the kind permission of Dr G. Elliot Smith and *The Lancet*"

THE PYGMIES

"Since writing the foregoing, by kind permission of the Manager of the London Hippodrome, *Mr Fred Trussell*, and *Colonel Harrison*, who brought them over from the forests of Ituri, in the Congo Free State, we have been able to examine the Pygmies here in London.

These Pygmies are primitive men—the little earth men. They are not negroes but are negroid, and many of their anatomical features show the near relationship they bear to the Pithecanthropos Erectus. The height of these Pygmies ranges from 1·378 metres, the tallest, to 1·158, the shortest; and they weigh from 7 stone, the heaviest, to 3 stone 7 pounds, the lightest. The average height of thirty-eight Akka Pygmies, from the Monbuttu country, is given as 1·378 metres by *Deniker*, and thirty Akkas, measured by *Emin Pasha*, gave an average height of 1·36 metres."

[From A. Churchward's Signs and Symbols of Primordial Man, p 14

XIIth Dynasty
(Cairo Museum

Left: Deposed Emperor Haile Selassie [Ethiopia]. **Center: Deceased daughter of Haile Selassie Ist.** **Murdered Emperor Lidj Yasu of Ethiopia.** **Right: Pharaoh Amonemhat II**

The "BEING" of Parmenides [132 D and Aristotle [META 16, 987 b 9] was a poor example to show for "THE EXISTENCE OF GOD" theory and doctrine of the Africans who taught about such in the MYSTERIES SYSTEM'S OSIRICA TEACHINGS, all of which was equally established upon "THE LAW OF OPPOSITES", and as expressed in "THE DIAGRAM OF THE LAW OF OPPOSITES" shown on the following page. Thus the STUDENTS in my course were introduced to both the works of Pharaoh Akhenaten [Amenhotep IVth] with respect to his own TEACHINGS about "THE FIRST MOVER WITHOUT MOVEMENT", and the Greeks VERSION they called:

"PROTON KINOUN AKINETON".

Professor William Turner, on page 141 of his HISTORY OF PHILSOPHY, described the above by means of Aristotle's[PHYSICS VIII 5, 256a, 192b 14; II 8, 199:14, 271a] explanation of "NATURE" to the "DEITY", the same as Professor Zeller tried to accomplish on page 61 c his own work, HISTORY OF PHILOSOPHY, with respect to Pamenides' earlier position - of which he tried to pass off to his fellow Greeks as his very own creation and development.

Although Diogenes Laertius [BOOK 9, pages 443-446] tried to justify the Greeks of questionable origin, and also those who were allegedly "INVOLVED IN CREATING PHILOSOPHICAL VALUES" for the DOCTRINE OF OPPOSITES, there could be no doubt that the Africans [BLACKS, NEGROES, BANTUS, et al] of Egypt had for thousands of years before the origin of the Europeans' City-State called PYRRHUS, ATHENIA or GREECE created the following THEORIES or PRINCIPLES that justify the a] OPPOSITE or CONTRARIES, b] CHANGE or TRANSMUTATION and, c] the LIFE FUNCTION of the universe caused by one or more of the Four Elements: AIR, FIRE, WATER, EARTH. For clarity the following DIAGRAM is presented once again. The reader should at this juncture try to figure some of the ramifications that affect his or her own life-style as a result of the laws and customs the Judaeo-Christian/Greek oriented societies ["Western Civlization"] adopted therefrom:

Elements:AIR, FIRE, WATER, EARTH

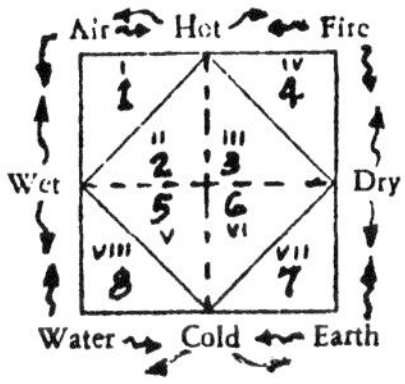

Qualities:HOT, WET, COLD, DRY

DIAGRAM OF THE FOUR QUALITIES AND FOUR ELEMENTS [1]
[Created and developed before Adam and Eve's story]

Professor George G. M. James gave us the simplest and most condensed explanation for the above DOCTRINE and DIAGRAM I am aware of; thus the following from page 81 of his major work - STOLEN LEGACY - [minus a single word edited]:

> The history of the following ancient theory of *"The Four Qualities and Four Elements"*, provides the world with the evidence of the Egyptian origin of the doctrines of (a) Opposites or Contraries, (b) Change or Transmutation and (c) the life and function of the universe is due to either of four elements: fire, or water, or earth or air.
>
> 1. This ancient theory was expressed by a diagram formed by outer and inner squares.
> 2. The corners of the outer square carried the names of the elements: fire, water, earth and air.
> 3. The corners of the inner square, being at the mid points of the sides of the outer square carried the four fundamental qualities, the hot, the dry, the cold and the wet.
> 4. The diagram explains that fire is hot and dry; earth is dry and cold; water is cold and wet; and air is wet and hot.

1. Directional arrows shown are by the author for clarity only; not by the Egyptians.

5. Accordingly water is an embodiment of cold and wet qualities, and when the cold quality is replaced by the hot quality, the element water is changed into the element air, with the wet and hot qualities.
6. Consequently, transmutation is definitely implied in the teaching of this symbol.
7. It is the oldest teaching of physical science and has been traced to the Egyptians, as far back as 5000 B. C.
8. It shows that Plato and Aristotle (who had been credited with the authorship of this teaching) derived their doctrines or portions of them from the Egyptians. (Rosicrucian Digest, May 1952, p. 175).

I suggest that the following works be given special attention if the reader wants to pursue further investigation in this subject. They should be read before attempting to decide whether the DOCTRINE expressed in this volume is RIGHT or WRONG due to your own religious or secular indoctrination:

C. H. Vail's ANCIENT MYSTERIES, Eva B. Sandford's MEDITERRANEAN WORLD, Max Muller's MYTHOLOGY OF EGYPT, H. Frankfurt's MEMPHITE THEOLOGY, Zeller's HISTORY OF PHILSOPHY, S. Clymer's FIRE PHILOSOPHY, E.A.Wallis Budge's [Translations] EGYPTIAN BOOK OF THE DEAD and PAPYRUS OF ANI, NEGATIVE CONFESSIONS, PYRAMID TEXTS, COFFIN TEXTS, B.D. Alexander's HISTORY OF PHILOSOPHY, J. Frazer's GOLDEN BOUGH [13 Vols.], W. Turner's HISTORY OF PHILOSOPHY, Plato's REPUBLIC, APOLOGY, and PHAEDO, Diogenes Laertius' BOOK I - IX, Rogers' HISTORY OF PHILOSOPHY, A. Weber's HISTORY OF PHILOSOPHY, J. Kendrick's ANCIENT EGYPT, G.G.M. James' STOLEN LEGACY, G. Massey's EGYPT THE LIGHT OF THE WORLD, and BOOK OF THE BEGINNING, PENTATEUCH [original Old Testament], KOJNE BIBLE [original New Testament], J.G. Jackson's MAN, GOD AND CIVILIZATION, H.W. Smith's MAN AND HIS GODS, Y. ben-Jochannan's AFRICA: MOTHER OF "WESTERN CIVILIZATION," BLACK MAN OF THE NILE AND HIS FAMILY, THE BLACK MAN'S RELIGION [3 Vols.], and J. Hasting's ENCYCLOPAEDIA OF RELIGION AND ETHICS [8 Vols.].

There should be no doubt left in the reader's mind as to why it has become necessary in WHITE ACADEMIA to remove all of the so-called "NEGROES, BANTUS, SUDANICS, AFRICANS SOUTH OF THE SAHARA," etc. [indigenous Africans] from North, East and Central "Africa's" HISTORY and HERITAGE in the past; but more specifically of today when "BLACK PEOPLE" everywhere are reading works such as this volume depicting the roles their ancestors played all over Alkebu-lan ["Africa" according to the Greeks], Asia and Europe in creating most of the CONCEPTS, THEORIES, DOCTRINES and PHILOSOPHI-

CAL TEACHINGS so many have since labeled "WESTERN CIVILIZATION" or "JUDAEO-CHRISTIAN ETHICS", etc., etc., etc. ad infinitum.

Where does all of this lead me as the PROFESSOR of all of the STUDENTS whose FINAL PAPERS in this volume I have exposed to the reading public; each for the first time in their rich and beautiful young BLACK life? Do we stop here? Do we change course in MID stream and pursue another major field dealing strictly with the SLAVE TRADE as so many of us are fully engaged? I must state, for myself, that these STUDENTS are prepared to enter any field in BLACK or WHITE ACADEMIA dealing with the "CARRY-OVERS" the African peoples of the Western Hemisphere inherrited from their Egyptian ancestors. And much more importantly, they are most competent to present said information in a much more simplified explanation in order for each and every BLACK PERSON to be able to read and digest easily. But, do they continue their own distinctly different discipline and only write occasionally an article or two in some obscure "SCHOLARLY MAGAZINE" or "NEWS-LETTER" especially geared to "SCHOLARS" exclusively; thereby denying the vast majority of the African-American [BLACK] People their precious knowledge about their [our] HISTORY and HERITAGE? Or, do they continue some major interest in the field of "AFRICANA STUDIES" and "RESEARCH" with the end result of bringing all of the knowledge they have learnt to the entire world community following their teaching of it to their own BLACK communities first? Only these STUDENTS, my three co-authors...

EVELYN WALKER, DOROTHY LEE COBB and CALVIN BIRDSONG...,

know the magical answer to all of the above questions with respect to themselves; and only they should make the decisions, or even answer the questions. For AFRICANA STUDIES, call it "BLACK STUDIES" if you prefer, is a field only those who are FANATICALLY DEDICATED TO THEIR AFRICAN ORIGIN should enter. Yet, the basic task is to RIGHT the WRONGS of centuries of European and European-American Christian Missionary activities, Jewish manipulations of the Holy Torah and other [so-called] "Holy Scriptures," and Moslem "Holy Wars" or "Jihads", all of which to remove every trace of the FIRST CONTRIBUTORS OF CIVILIZATION TO THE ENTIRE WORLD from said station to the lowest depth of degradation caused by the ACTS OF CULTURAL GENOCIDE African People still suffer at the hands of those from Asia, Europe and European-America:

> This is the story of the Europeans and European-Americans encounter against their fellow human beings from Africa and African-America, all of which we call a "Confrontation."

CONCLUSION: by Yosef ben-Jochannan.

Obviously the STUDENTS engaged in this RESEARCH PROJECT have uncovered certain information which hithertofore each and everyone of us did not know about our own selves as an AFRICAN PEOPLE. Others following will uncover even more; with our help.

The conceptions displayed in the "FINAL PAPERS" with respect to THE THEOSOPHICAL and SCIENTIFIC ORIGIN of THE DIAGRAM OF THE LAW OF OPPOSITES are basic enough to enable all of us to read some of the TRUTHS involved in our ancient religious HOLY SCRIPTURES that were coopted and adopted by the ISRAELITES [Jews], CHRISTIANS and MOSLEMS for their own religion's HOLY BOOKS. I speak of these religious personalities as if JUDAISM, CHRISTIANITY and/or ISLAM are related to one's RACE, COLOR or ETHNIC GROUPING. This is due to the fact that it is in this context that the PENTATEUCH [Old Testament], KOINÊ BIBLE [New Testament] and/or HOLY QUR'AN are presented to African-Americans, most believing that:

"IF IT WAS NOT FOR SLAVERY WE [African people] WOULD NEVER HAVE BEEN JEWS OR CHRISTIANS;"

of course the thought of ever being "MOSLEMS" almost frightens most of us to death's door.

The STUDENTS examination of such works as the so-called "EGYPTIAN BOOK OF THE DEAD and PAPYRUS OF ANI," TEACHINGS OF PHARAOH AMEN-EM-EOPE, NEGATIVE CONFESSIONS, PYRAMID TEXTS, COFFIN TEXTS, ETHIOPIAN CHRONICLES OF THE KINGS ["Kebra Negaste], etc., etc., etc. with respect to their ORIGINAL TEACHINGS adopted by all of the [so-called] JUDAEO-CHRISTIAN and JEWISH sects gave them a first-hand view and understanding why books such as these have been SUPPRESSED by theologians and other religious leaders. Their introduction to the LOST BOOKS OF THE BIBLE and FORGOTTEN BOOKS OF EDEN, AQUARIAN GOSPEL, REPORTS OF THE NICENE CONFERENCE OF BISHOPS, CONFERENCE OF TRENT, CONFERENCE OF ANTIOCH, WORKS BY St. Augustine, St. Cyprian and Tertullian, etc., allowed them to realize that the theory or allegory about the "IMMACULATE CONCEPTION" and "VIRGIN BIRTH OF JESUS" was common to at least "SIXTEEN CRUCIFIED SAVIORS" before the Christians' GOD; and that the story of ISIS and HORUS was the first of all of them.

It is unlikely that these STUDENTS would have been introduced to these works in any course other than by an accident. Thus it is that not only RESEARCH SKILLS are being sharpened by these STUDENTS, but also a vast amount of information and documents are revealed to them which challenge the authenticity of the teachings and claims about a distinct [so-called] "GREEK PHILOSOPHY," JUDAISM, CHRISTIANITY, ISLAM, etc. which have no [so-called]"BLACK AFRICAN" background and/or origin.

Professor George G. M. James' STOLEN LEGACY, Count C. F. Volney's RUINS OF EMPIRE and Sir Godfrey Higgins' ANACALYPSIS [2 vols], joined with Gerald Massey's BOOK OF THE BEGINNINGS [2 vols] and EGYPT THE LIGHT OF THE WORLD [2 vols], along with Dr. Albert Churchward's SIGNS AND SYMBOLS OF PRIMORDIAL MAN, ARCANA OF FREEMASONRY, etc., all of these classical works made the STUDENTS understand Sir Edward Hertslett's MAP OF AFRICA BY TREATY [3 vols] official documentation of the role of the United States of America and the other thirteen imperialist powers engaged in the PARTITION and COLONIZATION of the continent of "Africa," even though most of the professors of AMERICAN HISTORY and POLITICAL SCIENCE have constantly insisted that:

> THE UNITED STATES OF AMERICA TOOK NO ACTIVE PART IN THE COLONIZATION OF AFRICA OR THE DOMINATION OF ITS PEOPLE..., etc.

If it was at all possible for everyone of the STUDENTS to take at least one course in this area of AFRICANA STUDIES there would be such a CULTURAL REVOLUTION it would be literally impossible to pass off the current LILY WHITE GOLDEN HAIR European "GOD" and SPOTLESSLY WHITE HEAVEN in any BLACK COMMUNITY where they and their fellow BLACKS reside without an outright protest about such and its creation by Micahelangelo for Pope Julius IVth in ca. 1511 C.E. [A.D.]. The same will be equally true about the "TEN COMMANDMENTS" and its alledged origin with "MOSES", other than its original "BLACK AFRICAN" source in the "NEGATIVE CONFESSIONS" that preceded the birth of the first Haribu [Israelite or Jew] - "ABRAHAM" - by more than 2340 years, muchless Moses.

This first venture has proven itself of major importance in the preparation of future research materials, and for lecturing techniques before other STUDENTS. The fact that the STUDENTS were not burdened by any demand from me for a specific amount of WORDS or PAGES to adequately cover their assignment allowed them greater ease in expression and creativity in their work; thus the difference in length of each "FINAL PAPER."

Note that the chronological order of appearance of the "PAPERS" has nothing to do with their quality or importance. This I did intentionally, solely to avoid undue influence on the reader. You be your own judge if you believe that all STUDENT performances must be rated in terms of a competition between "F" to "A" etc. Let me hasten to say; I do not so believe.

The uniqueness of my 15,000 volumes private library made available to all added to the resources the STUDENTS used in their development and documentation of their thesis for their "FINAL PAPER." However, such PRIVATE LIBRARIES of the handful of African-Americans who are privileged to have them must become available to African-American [BLACK] Students and other Researchers, particularly those engaged in the process of reconstructing our AFRICAN HERITAGE, if we are to have adequately trained young BLACK SCHOLARS in the fields of EGYPTOLOGY, PHILOSOPHY, THEOLOGY, HISTORY, ART, SCIENCE, etc. from a BLACK PERSPECTIVE. These STUDENTS have now come to realize that except for the AUTHOR OLONZO SHOMBURG COLLECTION in the Cuntee Cullen Branch of the Public Library of the City of New York [Harlem, New York City, New York], others in a very few White colleges, and muchless so in Negro colleges, the greatest amount of volumes on, of and by African People are in PRIVATE LIBRARIES and/or COLLECTIONS. The known COLLECTIONS in the New York metropolitan area are: Professor John Henrike Clark's, Mr. Clarence Holt's, Professor Louis Michaux', Mrs.Sieffert's, Professor George E. Simmonds', and my own [Yosef ben-Jochannan's]; all of them located no more than a few blocks distance from the SCHOMBURG'S.

African or BLACK Studies courses must include indepth investigations into our ancient AFRICAN HISTORY in order to understand the original CREATION, DEVELOPMENT and CONTEMPORARY STATUS of our HERITAGE from our "motherland" - ALKEBU-LAN or "AFRICA" [the Greeks nomenclature for this continent]. For to rest all of our researches in the investigation of SLAVERY, the SLAVE TRADE and the SLAVE CULTURE will only perpetuate the popular myth propagandized by so-called "CHRISTIAN MISSIONARIES" from Europe and European-America along with their "NEGRO/COLORED" imitators:

> "THE NATIVES [meaning Africans] SOLD THEIR OWN PEOPLE INTO SLAVERY TO THE WHITE MAN...," etc., etc., etc.

When the TRUTH of the matter that is expressly documented in all of the basically historic works of the Africans are brought to the surface and it is shown that the so-called "NEGROES, BANTUS, PYGMIES, AFRICANS SOUTH OF THE SAHARA," et al were in fact the "CIVILIZERS OF THE FIRST EUROPEANS: GREEKS, ETRUSCANS AND ROMANS," et al these STUDENTS' "FINAL PAPERS" will take on much more meaningful dimensions. For from said beginning we have what is today called: "WESTERN" [European and/or White/Semitic] "CIVILIZATION." Strange! Ask any of my STUDENTS who have had at least ONE SEMESTER under my tutelege to document this fact; it will be done. The same TRUTH will show that it is information like the following which caused European and European-American academicians to claim African Origin before,and exclusive of the so-called "Black Africans:"

Ethiopia yields oldest human fossils

Discovery said to move human origins back to four million years ago

When—and where—was the beginning, the cradle of early man upon the earth? A succession of increasingly ancient discoveries has led some anthropologists to the point of virtually suspending their judgment, as more and more primitive examples of genus *Homo* push farther back the curtain of time. The latest addition to the growing line, announced last week in Ethiopia, shows the grounds for such conservatism, as it promises to extend human lineage as far back as four million years.

The finds—a complete upper jaw, half of another upper jaw and half a lower jaw, all with teeth—were found on Oct. 17 and 18 by Alemeyu Asfew of the Ethiopian Antiquities Commission, a member of the four-nation Afar Research Expedition. Working with D. Carl Johanson of Case Western Reserve University in Cleveland and Maurice Taieb of the French National Center for Scientific Research, he spotted the bones lying on the surface at a volcanic deposit on the Hadar, a tributary of the Awash River between the towns of Dessie and Assab in north-central Ethiopia.

The bones were in a stratigraphic level some 150 feet beneath, and thus probably much older than, a volcanic layer which has been dated (by the potassium-argon method) at from 3.01 to 3.25 million years old.

Further signs come from animal remains also found in the fossil-rich Hadar region, which is a virtual paleontologist's paradise. The Afar paleontologists have compared some of these animal fossils with well-dated samples from other sites in the East African Rift Valley System, and believe the Hadar animal samples to be at least four million years old. Because some of the animal samples were found in the same stratum as the man-like fossils, the researchers believe them to be of similar ages.

If substantiated, the Hadar find could indeed extend knowledge of man's origins back to previously unsuspected depths of the past. The small size of the teeth in the jawbones, hypothesizes Johanson, may well mean that genus *Homo* was "walking, eating meat and probably using tools, perhaps bones, to kill animals" as much as four million years ago. There is even the possibility, Johanson says, that he had "some kind of social cooperation and some sort of communication system."

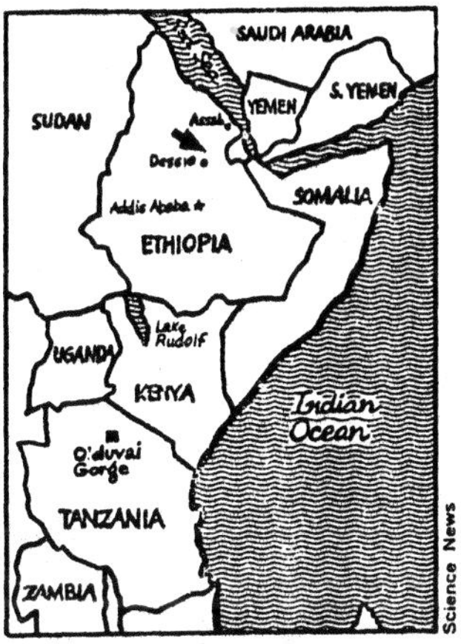

Fossil find in north-central Ethiopia.

The portent of the new discovery for anthropology is immense, although likely to be controversial. While speaking in terms such as "unparalleled," "exciting," and "a major revolution in all previous thinking," Johanson and his colleagues acknowledge that the bones may be "perhaps the most provocative human fossils ever discovered on the African continent. . . . It is certain," they admit, "that anthropologists from all over the world will meet these discoveries with extreme controversy and amazement."

Controversy is nothing new to anthropology, even without hoaxes such as the fabricated "Piltdown man." Remains from Olduvai Gorge in Tanzania and Lake Rudolf in Kenya, found by Louis S. B. Leakey and his son Richard, were dated by the Leakeys at from 2 to 2.6 million years, and the older dating is still the object of heated dispute, as is the question of whether the fossils are indeed those of genus *Homo*, thought of as the "true man," or of genus *Australopithecus*, a "near man."

Late last year, Johanson discovered some man-like, three-million-year-old bones, but determined that they belonged to *Australopithecus*. Nonetheless, the similarities between *Australopithecus* and *Homo* are enough that Johanson called his find "absolute, concrete evidence that our ancestors walked on two legs over three million years ago" (SN: 2/16/74, p. 103).

That find, which was in the Awash valley region that includes the Hadar rather than in the lower part of the Rift where the Leakeys' major discoveries were made, further supports a possibility advocated already by Richard Leakey. If *Australopithecus* lived in the same region occupied a million years before by the more highly evolved genus *Homo*, suggest Johanson and his Afar colleagues, it seems likely that the "true man" and the "near man" lived in the area at the same time.

Even so, the latest find is exciting enough on its own. "These specimens," the researchers maintain, "clearly exhibit traits which must be considered as indicative of the genus *Homo*. Taken together they represent the most complete remains of this genus from anywhere in the world at a very ancient time. All previous theories of the origin of the lineage which lead to modern man must now be totally revised. We must throw out many existing theories and consider the possibility that man's origins go back to well over four million years."

The researchers have, however, suggested one possibility that will almost certainly add controversy to an already controversial field. The part of the Awash valley where the finds were made is little more than 100 miles from the Red Sea and a near land bridge to the Middle East. A backwards chronology, from Louis Leakey's two-million-year-old find in Tanzania to his son's 2.6-million-year-old find northward in Kenya to the latest three- and four-million-year-old fossils all the way up in Ethiopia, suggest to the Afar team what they admit is a "revolutionary postulate." The cradle of humanity, they hypothesize (in the most tentative terms), may, in fact, be on the other side of that bridge, in the Middle East. Richard Leakey and others (doubtless including many of the Afar researchers) believe man's origins to lie in Africa. But the other possibility—and a revolutionary one it would certainly be—is there. □

THICK LIPS, BROAD NOSE, KINKY HAIR, BURNT SKIN, ETC.; BUT TOO SHORT FOR "NEGROES;" THEY ARE "BLANQUITOS" or "LITTLE WHITES"? ASK HALLET HOW!

1 2 3 4

5 6 7 8

All of the pictures below except numbers 6 and 9 were taken by Hallet; and they are Hutus or Twas - colonialist terms "PYGMIES" or "PYGMY." Number 6 are Ghanians; number 9 Ethiopians - colonialist scholarship's "Semites" and/or "Hamites." Strange! How do they differ to BLACKS in the U.S.A. and **other** parts of "Africa"? They are "Caucasians"? Ask Hallet how is this possible; Churchward also. How?

To say that there is no RACISM involved in "OBJECTIVE SCHOLARSHIP," if there is such a phenomena as being "OBJECTIVE" when one is examining artifacts, documents, people, places and things related to one's own self, will be dishonest on the part of any type of "PROFESSOR" who says that the so-called "SEMITES, HAMITES, CAUCASOIDS, NILOTS, PYGMIES," etc. shown on the preceding pages of this volume are of the same "RACE" as the man - Jean-Pierre Hallet [author of PYGMY KITABU, New York, 1975] - in the center of page 58 - CAUCASIAN! For example Hallet and his co-author Alex Pelle wrote the following on pages 12 - 13 in the above mentioned book:

Negrillos—"little blacks" or "little Negroes." The word was coined by nineteenth-century anthropologists who theorized, without benefit of evidence, that the Pygmies were degenerate, dwarfish or even shrunken Negroes. This ill-informed belief, which simultaneously libels the Pygmy and Negro branches of mankind, survives today in direct contradiction to the facts, which were thus summarized by Dr. Jean Leyder, the former administrator of the Ubangi district in the northwest Congo:

> The Pygmy constitutes a totally distinctive race, strikingly different from the Negro.
> The Pygmy is not a degenerate Negro.
> The Negro is not a Pygmy grown larger.
> The Pygmy has been thus for thousands of years: on a monument of ancient Egypt, the Egyptologist Mariette found engraved the portrait and the name of a Pygmy, "Akka," who resembled the present-day Aka Pygmies of Uele. If the strikingly original physical constitution of the Pygmies had been the result of degeneration, the Pygmy race would have disappeared a long time ago. Instead their historic existence as a population of small stature is attested to in Central Africa for millennia. And far from being a declining race, the Pygmies of the Belgian Congo are at present one of the healthiest, most vigorous, most prolific peoples . . . Grave dangers may have recently menaced their survival; these dangers come, however, from the exterior and not from the race itself.
> Medically speaking, the Pygmy is not a dwarf (degenerate, sterile).
> In brief, the Pygmies are not abnormal people. They constitute a race of normally small stature, a strongly individualized race that is entirely distinct from the Negroes . . .
> The prominent brows, the thin lips, testify to a primordial connection with the Europeans . . .[1]

Like the Pygmies, Caucasians or whites are very ancient residents of the so-called Dark Continent. Negroes are not. Dr. Sonia Cole discussed this topic in *The Prehistory of East Africa:* "There were apparently three basic stocks in Africa before the appearance of the Negro: the proto-Australoids with heavy browridges (typified by Rhodesian man, Hopefield man, and Eyasi man); the proto-Bushmanoids; and the proto-Caucasoids, or, to give them a more local but less accurate name, the proto-Hamites . . . All the Upper Paleolithic peoples of Kenya were of Caucasoid or proto-Hamitic stock; they are represented by the Gamble's Cave and Naivasha skeletons as well as the skeleton from Olduvai in northern Tanganyika." [2]

In present-day East Africa, there are many mixed Hamite/Negro tribes. The famous Masai people of Kenya and Tanzania are very dark-skinned folk who sometimes have almost Grecian profiles. The tall Tutsi* or "Watusi" of Rwanda and Burundi apparently represent another Caucasoid–Negro cross; their non-Negroid traits include big hooked noses of the type usually described as Semitic. In his exhaustive study of the "Watusi," R. Bourgeois explained that eastern and southern Africa present "three types of fossil men who can easily be considered as ancestors of the Bushmen, Pygmies and present-day hybrid Hamite–Blacks." What did he have to say about the Negroes? "As surprising as it may seem, it is outside the area of contemporary Black Africa that one finds fossil specimens approaching the Negroes . . ." [3]

Some scholars have theorized that the Negroes originated elsewhere and arrived in Africa at some unknown date, in the manner of the Indo-European tribes who invaded India and the Yankee colonists who invaded North America.

[1] Jean Leyder, "Les Pygmées du Congo Belge," from the *Bulletin de la Société Royale Belge de Géographie*, No. 3-4 (Brussels, 1934), pp. 7-8, 11.

[2] Sonia Cole, *The Prehistory of East Africa* (Penguin Books, 1954), pp. 111, 113.

*In this work, all ethnic names are given without prefixes (as suggested by the International African Institute). This will avoid any ambiguity and confusion caused by the varying forms of tribal prefixes (as "Watusi," BaTutsi, etc.).

[3] R. Bourgeois, *Banyarwanda et Barundi* (Brussels, 1957), Vol. 1, p. 16.

The type of "OBJECTIVE SCHOLARSHIP" we see in Hallet/Pelle's words is common to the entire "ACADEMIC COMMUNITY" of the United States of America. What is so disturbing about it all is that the so-called "NEGRO ACADEMICIANS" feel obliged to echo the same GENOCIDAL racism under the protection of "ACADEMIC COMMONALITY." But why? WHY would a "NEGRO/COLORED [supposedly Black] SCHOLAR" feel compelled to echo this type of racism? Because so very few of us BLACK [African-American] SCHOLARS are willing to become involve in PRIMARY RESEARCH and accept our own BLACK AUTHORITY. Primarily the matter is also controlled by the fact that we are afraid of not being accepted by our fellow WHITE COLLEAGUES who may block our way when we are applying to any WHITE INSTITUTION for a position and/or grant; this being equally true for tenure.

The answer to all of this rests directly in the hands of the up-and-coming YOUNG BLACK SCHOLARS who will be coming out of AFRICAN STUDIES and RESEARCH programs; particularly from formerly "NEGRO INSTITUTIONS" turned "BLACK." But these institutions must equally have their own PUBLISHING HOUSES; yet not necessarily their own PRINTING PLANTS; as it is at the PUBLISHERS that most of the manuscripts submitted by BLACK-MINDED African, African-American and African-Caribbean SCHOLARS must go through all sorts of changes, to the extent that they are not recognizable following the EDITORS use of their red marks of rejection. It is equally at this point that the WHITE CONSULTANT, who is also the self-proclaimed "AUTHORITY ON AFRICA" and "AFRICAN PEOPLE," will be given the censors' power of DECIDING WHAT IS RIGHT and/or WRONG about one's entire thesis, irrespective of the PRIMARY DOCUMENTATION one has submitted. This "AUTHORITY'S" lack of knowledge of the FACTS and DOCUMENTATION presented means absolutely nothing to the PUBLISHER. Worst of all; calling upon any "NEGRO AUTHORITY" will not help, as practically ALL of the so-called "NEGRO/COLORED/BLACK AUTHORITIES" used by WHITE PUBLISHERS are subjected to the "APPROVAL" of the WHITE CONSULTANT or EDITOR-IN-CHIEF, etc., etc., etc. ad infinitum.

I have made all of this known to my STUDENTS. In so doing, I have also told them about the type of EXCUSES common in the PUBLISHING INDUSTRY which African-American AUTHORS have to contend with. Of course they are also made aware of the very few BLACK PUBLISHING HOUSES there are at present; and about their LIMITED area of circulation due to unavailable cash. They have equally been advised that GRANTS, UNDERWRITERS, SPONSORS..., etc. which normally exist through WHITE PHILANTHROPICAL INSTITUTIONS and WHITE INDIVIDUALS are very rare indeed from BLACK SOURCES - rich or poor.

It is more than safe to say that COURSE AS and RC 510 taught by Visiting Professor Yosef ben-Jochannan has been a total EXPERIENCE not only in "HISTORIOGRAPHY AND SOURCE" [its tittle], but definitely also in terms of the entire PUBLISHING INDUSTRY and its effect upon the BLACK SCHOLAR, his or her MANUSCRIPT, and also the BLACK INTERPRETATION being made WHITE by the PUBLISHER'S "AUTHORITIES".

Some how all of the centers and institutions involved with AFRICANA STUDIES and RESEARCH must be in the position to PUBLISH their talented YOUNG BLACK SCHOLARS' works. But it is incumbent upon WEALTHY BLACKS to make GRANTS and other GIFTS to BLACK ACADEMICIANS and RESEARCHERS possible. For it is no doubt that:

"HE WHO PAYS THE FIDDLER CALLS THE TUNE."

Certainly HE WHO MAKES THE GRANTS EXACTS THE CONDITIONS FOR SAME. The FACTS and the RESULTS are self-evident in this volume. Those who had doubts, and there are many on all sides of the COLOR LINE, about AFRICANA or BLACK STUDIES can observe for themselves the INJUSTICE they have so long brought to bare upon those of US who continue turning out the type of YOUNG BLACK SCHOLARS who wrote what we read in this volume. But these are only a DROP IN THE BUCKET. There are litterally thousands of them waiting to be unwrapped. Their "SCHOLARSHIP" must be added to the greats like Dr. W.E.B. DuBois, Dr. Carter G. Woodson, Joel A. Rogers, Dr. Willis Huggins, Dr. X. Springer, Professor John Henrike Clark, Dr.G. Osei, Professor G. G. M. James, Professor C.L.R. James, Dr. C. Eric Lincoln, Dr. C.H. Cone, Dr. Vincent Harding, and many thousands more living and deceased from this side of the Atlantic and Pacific oceans; not even to mention those from the other side in the motherland - Alkebu-lan! For it is only when we, AFRICAN-AMERICANS OF BLACK ACADEMIA, recognize our own SCHOLARS will they be TRULY AUTHORITY on OURSELVES, OUR HISTORY, OUR MOTHERLAND, and of course OUR RELIGION and GOD. All of the ETHNIC, RACIAL, RELIGIOUS and NATIONAL peoples of the entire Planet EARTH decide who will be their AUTHORITY. And without a solitary exception; IT IS ALWAYS ONE OF THEIR VERY OWN. Why should the African-[BLACK]-American, African-Caribbean and African ACADEMICIANS be the only exception?

It is hoped that the READER of this volume will express his and/or her CONSTRUCTIVE criticisms to the professor, students and adminsitrators whose activities made this what we believe to be only the FIRST GIANT STEP to a great future in AFRICAN, AFRICAN-AMERICAN and AFRICAN-CARIBBEAN HISTORY, CULTURE and HERITAGE publications between STUDENTS, their TEACHING PROFESSORS and RESEARCH PROFESSORS, etc.

INDEXED CITATIONS OF SOURCES IN THE TEXTBOOK:[1]

Page No.	Description of Citation and Commentary	Page No. Tex
1 - 17	Foundations of the Judaeo-Christian-Islamic religions and so-called "Greek Philosophy"..	313 - 33
22	Man and his "DEIFICATION" theories, etc..........................	313 - 31
22	Origin of the "MYSTERIES SYSTEM" and its functions...............	251 - 25
22	Detailing the "DIAGRAM OF THE LAW OF OPPOSITES".............	319 - 32
22	Comparative listing of JESUS/OSIRIS'names, etc....................	124 - 12
22	Chronological list of the "PHARAOHS" and "DYNASTIES"	139 - 16
22	Source of the so-called "TEN COMMANDMENTS".....................	341 - 36
23	Views about a "SUPREME BEING" or "GREATEST INTELIGENCE"....	313 - 31
23	Source of the "PHILOSOPHICAL THEORIES" from the Nile Valley High-Cultures as adopted and plagiarized by the so-called "GREEK PHILOSOPHERS" - from Thales to Aristotle, et al..................	313 - 33
23	"RACIAL TYPES" of Greco-Roman Citizens hithertofore never publicized as either Greek and/or Roman "NEGROES", etc.............	71 - 72
24	The "POLYTHEISTIC GODS" of the Hall Of The Gods................	124 - 12
24	"DOCTRINE OF THE NOUS and SONUM," etc........................	314 - 31
25	The so-called "PYTHAGOREAN THEORY" and its Alkebu-lan origin [review page 5, first paragraph]......................................	332 - 33
25	Pyramids and their "MASONIFIED CALCULATIONS" that created the base concepts for theosophy and theology..............................	205 - 22
25	The "NUMEROLOGY OF THE DIAGRAM OF OPPOSITES," etc.........	215 - 21
25	"METAPHYSICS" and "MENTAPHYSICS," etc........................	327 - 33
26	Birth, Death, Resurrection and Immortality, etc....................	313 - 31
26	Jesus "the Christ" and Osiris as JESUS and HORUS nursing on their mother's breast..	373 - 37
26	The African and his or her "DIVINE LAW" passed down to Europeans...	320 - 32
28	"GOOD" or "GOD, BAD" or "EVIL" [Devil], etc......................	321 - 32
29	Masonified identification of "IMMORTALITY": Son Of Light, etc.......	314 - 31
29	The Mysteries System and its ruined "GRAND LODGE, etc............	251 - 25
29	Esoteric and Exoteric PHILOSOPHICAL CONCEPTS examined.........	333 - 33

1. The page numbers at the right represent those in the textbook used in the Course, Y. ben-Jochannan's BLACK MAN OF THE NILE AND HIS FAMILY; those at the left are of this volume. Citations listed chronologically according to appearance in this volume.

[indexed citations continued]

Page No.	Description of Citation and Commentory	Page No. Text
29	Biblical Characters, Dates and Chronology of ideological concepts in ancient religion..	213 - 219
29	"PHALLIC SYMBOLISM" and the PYRAMIDS, OBELISKS, STALAE, CANDACES, SPHINXES, etc..	184 - 194
29	Sex, Astronomy, Astrology, Theology, etc. along the Nile Valley, etc..	
30	The ANKH, CROSS and GRAMADON in Ta-Merry, etc................	361 - 372
31	The Grand Lodge of Luxor where the Greeks received their first concepts of "PHILOSOPHY" created by the Nile Valley and Great Lakes indigenous Africans, et al..	327 - 338
31	"NUMBERS" and their origin in Alkebu-lan.........................	205 - 210
34	The "KA" and "BA" as Spirits, Souls and Salvation, etc..............	322 - 323
34	Chronology of the HARIBU FATHERS or PATRIARCHS...............	213 - 218
34	Death Scene and "IMMORTALITY": Trial of Scribe Ani, etc...........	122 - 123
35	The "WORLD OF GENESIS" and "ADAM" through maps..............	195 - 197
35	YAHWEH and RA in history...	343 - 344
36	JUDGMENT SCENE compared to the HEREAFTER..................	122 - 123
36	Ethiopia/Egypt/Sudan/Meröe/Puanit, etc. - the NILE VALLEY........	137 - 138
38	The "WINTER SOLTICE" explained....................................	209 - 227
39	"HIGH-CULTURES" and other words explained in a "GLOSSARY"......	120 - 137
41 - 42	"CHRISTIANITY" and its Alkebu-lan ["African"] origins, etc..........	375 - 377
41 - 43	"MYSTERIES SYSTEM" analysis of "TRANSMUTATION," etc.........	322 - 323
44	"THE FEELING CHILD" nursing on its mother's breast...............	373 - 374
44	Isis the "FERTILITY GODESS" and HUMAN MOTHER OF GOD - Horus or Osiris, et al..	200, 379

Note: The students were previliged to equally have at their convenience five of my other works as added sources for details and documentation - AFRICA: MOTHER OF "WESTERN CIVILIZATION," AFRICAN ORIGINS OF THE MAJOR "WESTERN RELIGIONS" - JUDAISM, CHRISTIANITY, and ISLAM, etc....[vol. I], THE BLACK MAN'S RELIGION [vol. II, III, etc. - 3 vols. under one cover], and CULTURAL GENOCIDE IN THE BLACK AND AFRICAN STUDIES CURRICULUM. Having these works at the reader's convenience will greatly enhance his or her understanding of this volume.

Rear cover under same copyright provisions as the front cover and other portions of the entire text of this volume. Symbols and pictures in the collage are taken from many of my other works.

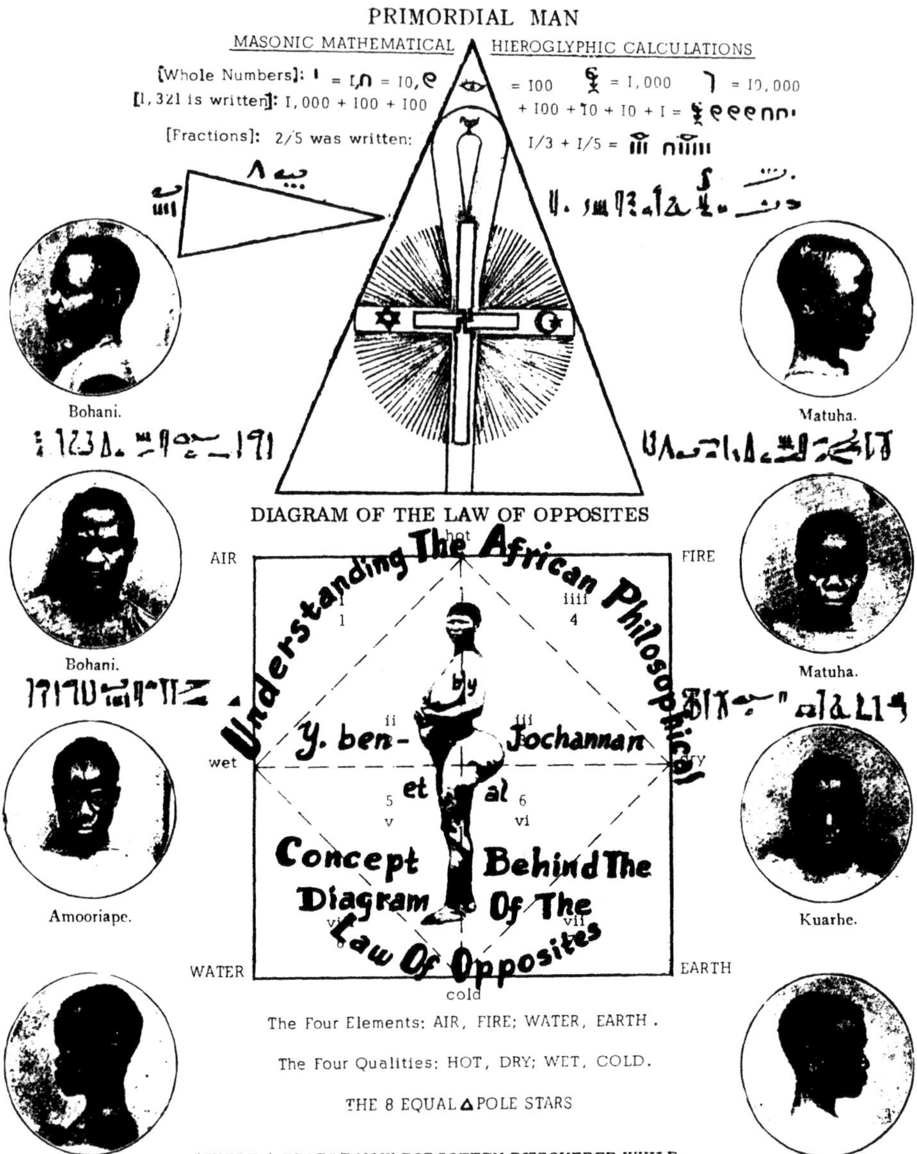

Amooriape.

Kuarhe.

"THERE A PEOPLE NOW FORGOTTEN DISCOVERED WHILE OTHERS WERE YET BARBARIANS, THE ELEMENTS OF THE ARTS AND SCIENCES. A RACE OF MEN NOW REJECTED FOR THEIR SABLE SKIN AND FRIZZLED HAIR, FOUNDED ON THE STUDY OF THE LAWS OF NATURE THOSE CIVIL AND RELIGIOUS SYSTEMS WHICH STILL GOVERN THE UNIVERSE."

PERSONAL NOTES

PERSONAL NOTES

Titles by Yosef ben-Jochannan Available from Black Classic Press

Africa Mother of Western Civilization

Dr. Ben examines the African foundations of Western civilization. In lecture/essay format, he identifies and corrects myths about the inferiority and primitiveness of the indigenous African people and their descendants. He mentions many authorities on Africa and their works, and proves how they are racist in intent.
ISBN 0-933121-25-3. 1971*, 1988. 750 pp. illus. Paper. $34.95.

Black Man of the Nile

In a masterful and unique manner, Dr. Ben uses *Black Man of the Nile* to challenge and expose "Europeanized" African history. He reveals distortion after distortion made in the long record of African contributions to world civilization. Once these distortions are exposed, he attacks them with a vengeance, and provides a spellbinding corrective lesson.
ISBN 0-933121-26-1. 1972*, 1989. 381 pp. illus. Paper. $24.95.

A Chronology of the Bible: Challenge to the Standard Version

Chronology documents the African origins of Judaism, Christianity, and Islam. Dr. Ben traces some of the significant influences, developments, and people that have shaped and provided the foundation for the holy books used in these religions.
ISBN 0-933121-28-8. 1972*, 1995. 24 pp. Paper. $4.00.

Cultural Genocide in the Black and African Studies Curriculum

As Black and African studies programs emerged in the early 1970's, the question of who has the right and responsibility to determine course content and curriculum also emerged. In 1972, Dr. Ben's critique on this subject was published as *Cultural Genocide in the Black and African Studies Curriculum.* It has been republished several times since then and its topic has remained timely and unresolved.
ISBN 1-57478-022-0. 1972*, 2004. 150 pp. Paper. $14.95.

Our Black Seminarians and Black Clergy Without a Black Theology

In *Black Seminarians,* Dr. Ben outlines sources of Black theology before Judaism, Christianity, and Islam and shows how their ideas, practices, and concepts were already old in Africa before Europe was born. Introduction by John Henrik Clarke.
ISBN 0-933121-62-8. 1978*, 1998. 109 pp. Paper. $14.95.

We the Black Jews

Dr. Ben destroys the myth of a "white Jewish race" and the bigotry that has deni the existence of an African Jewish culture. He establishes the legitimacy contemporary Black Jewish culture in Africa and the diaspora and predates i origin before ancient Nile Valley civilizations. This work provides insight a historical relevance to the current discussion of Jewish and Black cultur relationships.
ISBN 0-933121-40-7. 1983*, 1993. 408 pp. illus. Paper. $24.95.

The Black Man's Religion

Now available in three volumes

African Origins of the Major Western Religions

In volume one, Dr. Ben critically examines the history, beliefs, and myths tha are the foundation of Judaism, Christianity, and Islam. The Black Classic Pres edition is a facsimile edition, with an added index and extended bibliography.
ISBN 0-933121-29-6. 1970*, 1991. 363 pp. Paper. $24.95.

The Myth of Exodus and Genesis and the Exclusion of Their African Origins

In volume two, Dr. Ben highlights the often overlooked African influences an roots of the world's major religions.
ISBN 0-933121-76-8. 1974*, 2002. 74 pp. Paper. $14.95.

The Need for a Black Bible

This third volume is an invaluable resource for anyone seeking to gain a bette understanding of belief systems in the Western world.
ISBN 0-933121-58-X. 1974*, 2002. 120 pp. Paper. $16.95.

To order, send a check or money order to:

Black Classic Press
P.O. Box 13414
Baltimore, MD 21203-3414

Include $5 for shipping and handling, and $.50 for each additional book ordered. Credit card orders call: 1-800-476-8870
For additional titles, please visit our website at www.blackclassic.com

**Indicates first year published*